Reiki

A Guide to Your Practice

of

Reiki Energy Healing

To:

Gabriel

The Reiki Healing Precepts

Just for today,
I release all anger.
Today feel no anger.

Just for today,
I release all worry.
Have no worries.

I show gratitude for all my many blessings.
Feel gratitude.

I earn my living with integrity.
Show diligence in your undertaking.

I honor every living thing.
Treat others with kindness.

MEDITATION ON REIKI KANJI

Reiki

At the end of my classes I offer this meditation on the Reiki kanji. With thanks to Fokke Brink, a Reiki Master who taught me the art of Sumi Calligraphy and drew the original of this calligraphy which hangs in my Reiki room.

Japanese in its written form is a picture language - and "a picture is worth a thousand words". The characters/images which hold the meaning are interpreted in the eye, and understanding, of the beholder. This is another meditation I have never written down before, preferring to go with the feeling of the moment as I share the meanings. I'll do my best to capture the flow.

REI - Universal Energy

The first character in REI is "RAIN" and is made up of a line at the top, a large curved line and several short lines.

"Under heaven" - the straight line at the top of a character divides heaven and earth. The energy comes down (straight line down) through the "clouds of illusion" - the large curved line shows a rain cloud, the four short lines depict raindrops. When it is a rainy day we often say, "There is no sun", when of course there is a sun, it is simply obscured by the heavy clouds in our particular area of the world. Sometimes our problems are so large and in our face they are like the clouds obscuring the sun.

The second character is 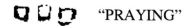 "PRAYING"

The energy comes down because the people are praying [asking, a willingness to receive] - one square represents a mouth, and would be a person speaking. Two squares mean a conversation - two people speaking. Three squares represents praying. Four would be a conference. And that is as far as it goes.

The third character is "MAGIC"

Under heaven the energy comes down to the earth - the strong line of the base of the character represents the earth - because the shaman are dancing [conscious motion].

So, "rain" (without which we wouldn't have life here on the earth plane), "praying/asking" (conversation with the divine, whatever you perceive that to be) and "magic" (miracles, events beyond logical understanding) come together to express the meaning of REI - Universal Life Energy. I often think of this as sight (through the clouds of illusion), sacred sound (praying/asking), and the gesture of putting hands on (intentional motion/the shaman dancing), which are three ways of activating Reiki in the second level.

KI - Personal Energy

The three lines at the top are clouds again, but a different kind, you could think of them as like a mist that is gently absorbed by the earth.

The long heavy line represents the seeming solid crust of the earth. Now the earth looks solid, and we even refer to it as such, and it really isn't very solid - trees and grass and flowers grow up through it. Our bodies aren't as solid as we like to think, either. If you put a dot at the top left hand corner of this page you are reading, and that dot represented the nucleus of an atom, the nearest electron would be at the lower right hand corner of the page. That is a considerable amount of empty space, proportionately speaking. Atoms are held together by centrifugal force (energy - surprise!).

Inside the seeming solid crust of the earth is the "seed" (ki). A cross with four dots would denote a farmer's fields. Two semi-circles with a line in the middle and band across would show "harvest" - a sheaf of wheat or rice harvest = seed. (isn't that great?) This is the "seed" of ourselves.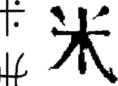

When the rain (Reiki energy) seeps through the seeming solid crust of the earth (our own bodies) and enters the seed - ki (ki means our person, personal energy), nothing can stop the power of growth. I know you have seen plants growing through a crack in the cement. It is the same for us. As we receive Universal Energy - even if it is only through a crack in our veneer - such is the power of our personal growth and transformation.

Rei = Universal Life Energy   brought through

Ki = Personal Energy   for the purposes of healing.

This is *ReiKi*.

Table of Contents

Table of Contents - Continued

ACKNOWLEDGMENTS

This is the page you usually skip, right? I promise to be interesting, just in case.

Linda Keiser Mardis is simply an awesome teacher, no matter the subject. I am forever grateful that she is my initiating Master in Reiki. I was way at the back, doing the bibliography, when I realized that I don't have titles to list and quote to give Linda the credit she deserves. Reiki was an entirely oral tradition when she shared it with me. Linda invited me into her classes on Reiki and other things, into her home and heart for the three years before and all the years since my initiation as a teaching Master. She introduced me to many of the Masters and teachers who have contributed so richly to my life and my path. And even when she disagrees with me, she always supports me to recognize and act on my own truth. Her integrity speaks for itself, and is a beacon to others. Everything I teach has an essence of Linda within. God/Goddess bless.

Lorie Borris is my sister in a lot of ways. We have held each other's hand through every stage of our lives since we met while studying with Linda. We have traveled, studied, shopped, been broke and rich, and figured out the seven things we need to know about anything together, including the meaning of life. Josephine Miranda, another sister Master, is our calm and steady support, sends Reiki everywhere all the time, speaks her truth beautifully and "sleeps on" things very well. Blessings.

After each initiation in Reiki, the Master bows to the student and says something like, "I thank you for allowing me to be your teacher, and I especially thank you for teaching me." This is to acknowledge that we are all each other's teachers. I would like to thank some special people who began as my students, have continued to work closely with me (four now initiated Masters) and who have been instrumental in this book.

Randy Thomas Gearhart is a nationally certified addictions counselor. We met when he was seeking a more holistic approach to healing. He found it in Reiki. He is now a Master. Without Randy and the work we have done together around the world I would simply not be where I am today. Randy, thank God you actually read the travel guides! And thank you for all the miles we have travelled.

Jan Smith is also a counselor and now a Master. Jan, Randy and I were among the founding members of the North East Reiki Gathering, and have continued to work closely together in community service for the last seven years. Jan, thank you for so joyously sharing your expertise, your clear insights, your compassion and your constant loving support. You believe in me. And that is a gift beyond measure.

Carol von Kaenel, also now a Master, thank you for the urgings to and the example of writing down some of the healing lore. Carol took the teaching notes I kept over my years of training with Linda Keiser Mardis, my own additions since then, and her own experiences in training, and compiled these into a very professional guide. Carol you are wonderfully generous with your love, attention, skills, home(s) and resources for Reiki gatherings. You are a class act, my dear. And you knit beautifully.

I want to thank Heather Buglear, Reiki Master, and Peter Coates, who let me make their Portchester, Hampshire home my home and office as I actually got this book on paper. It lived in my head and heart for a long time. I carried a portable computer (thank you, Dave Miller) halfway around the world putting in bits and pieces. Heather let me use her office and her brand new computer to get it organized. Peter, ever polite and patient, translated computerese for me in England, Dave in America. Heather, thank you for organizing my life, which God knows is no easy task, cooking the meals and cleaning up while this got done. Thanks for all the trips to the printer, driving me around on the wrong side of the road, painting Kanjis, punching holes and guillotining pages into the wee hours. I can't find words to thank you for the rest.

Many thanks to Patricia Varney who has been helping me sort the paperwork in my life for several years. I never knew you had a secret life as an artist! The illustrations are wonderful, just like you.

Pam Smith, artist, author and counselor, served as editor for this book. Thank you for your hospitality as we worked on the rearrangements. You are both clear and gentle, a graceful combination. I am blessed by your friendship.

Dave Miller, now a Master, last but certainly not least called upon! deserves sainthood for unwavering patience in the face of endless remedial questions about the computer with its whims and wiles. He even makes house calls when necessary - a rare man indeed. And he was quite patient when he found a decorative magnet on my hard drive. My deepest gratitude for bringing a professional polish to this book for each printing - for your many hours of dedicated time and expertise, and for your continued support in communication Enterprises.

Thank you to all my students for being my teachers.

Namaste!

INTRODUCTION

Reiki is a hands-on experience. It cannot be learned or "gotten" from a book. To learn or receive Reiki a person attends a first level class or training with an initiated teaching Master, and receives four initiations or attunements to the energy along with instruction and practice time. Everything you need to know about practicing Reiki on yourself is contained in that class and in your own subsequent practice.

So then, why this book?

Because I find Reiki absolutely fascinating. I have since the minute I was introduced to it. I find the changes in myself when I practice Reiki fascinating, also the responses of other people when I share Reiki with them. I have practiced Reiki on everything from a race horse with a broken leg (and his trainer) to radish plants for a botany project, and a lot of humans in between. To know that healing is an innate ability, and to share that understanding with others has been the most beautiful and powerful blessing of my life.

I successfully resisted writing about Reiki for years, upholding the oral tradition through which it was given to me. I also understand the reasoning that once information is trapped in words on paper for some people it can cease to be a guide and may become rules, or even a substitute for a person's own experiences, practice, and knowing. Reiki cannot actually be captured or contained in words because in its beautifully simple essence it is about application - personal practice and experience.

Keeping this in mind, I also hear the call for readable information that exists outside a class framework. I clearly recall my own desire and even need for more about Reiki - more information, more stories about people's experiences in giving and receiving, teaching, learning, and simply sharing Reiki. I am a person who loves stories, and who learns from and through them, especially historical stories.

For some years I was one of just a few practitioners, and then the only teaching Master in New York State. It was sort of lonely. I remember being so grateful when Helen Haberly and Fran Brown wrote their books about Takata. For me these books have never been a substitute for classes or practice or sharing with other practitioners. They have been an enrichment, and a place for me to share experiences - to think more deeply about my own understandings as compared with what each person has written.

In my second decade of practice in Reiki, the Usui System of Natural Healing, I now see this book as an extension of my sharing of this healing art - to write down some of my personal experiences and understandings of this system, share some stories and some information I find interesting. I hope this book is an enrichment for you in your practice of the healing art of Reiki.

I trained in, have practiced (since April 14, 1985), and taught (since April 6, 1988) the Usui System of Natural Healing. My "lineage" is Mikao Usui, Chujiro Hayashi, Hawayo Takata, Phyllis Furumoto, Linda Keiser Mardis.

I want to make it clear that I do not speak for this system. What I offer you here is my experience and perspective gained through my practice, both personal and professional - sharing the Usui System of Natural Healing with people just like you all over the world.

There are three levels of training in the Usui System - first, second and master. The first level contains everything you need for personal practice. Reiki at each level is about individual practice: learning and understanding through your own experience, giving and receiving a peaceful, loving energy that brings balance to the body/mind/spirit entity and allows healing to naturally occur. To understand Reiki, experience it - put your hands on yourself (if you have been initiated), or pick up the telephone and make an appointment with an Usui System practitioner, or sign up for a class.

When I teach Reiki at the first level, there are only two things I ask my students to remember:

> 1. This is a hand, this is a body, this is Reiki.
> 2. Use it. Practice.

Almost everything else we talk about in class is merely entertainment for the left brain, keeping it busy so the right brain has a chance to remember something we all already know - how to heal ourselves and each other.

The Usui System of Natural Healing (as it was shared with me - there are other forms, more about that later) is the simplest, most effective, most user-friendly healing system I have ever encountered. It supports any other form of healing or therapy in that it brings balance to the body, facilitating, reminding, catalyzing and empowering the body to heal itself. The practice of Reiki has given me a container to hold and understand all my feelings about healing on the physical, emotional and spiritual levels. I make a promise in each of my classes - if I ever find anything simpler or more effective, I will personally write you all a letter and let you know what it is. In the meantime, the practice of Reiki has quite simply changed my life.

Welcome to Reiki! All blessings as you begin this portion of your path.

Namaste

Penelope Jewell
November, 1995

ABOUT THE AUTHOR

Every teaching Master has a story of how they came to Reiki. We usually share this story at the beginning of a class. The students get to know us as people who have used Reiki in our lives, and who speak from that experience: how the simple use of Reiki has enriched our lives and our way of being.

At the time I became acquainted with Reiki I had a small business in Saratoga Springs, New York. Saratoga Springs is both a college and a resort town, boasting healing springs and mineral baths, and horse racing for most of the year. The architecture is turn-of-the century Victorian, and the town motto is "Health, History and Horses." We are about as "small town" as you get, but we do have a contingent of people interested in psychic phenomena, and a fair number of ghosts from the turn of the century heyday - enough to be entertaining, anyway. I had been studying psychic phenomena and energetic healing for a number of years, I found it an interesting hobby.

When I first heard the word "Reiki" it was actually during a psychic reading. The reader said, "You are good with your hands, you will do something called 'Reiki'." I dutifully wrote the word down, funny I even knew how to spell it. I went to the library to look up "Reiki". There was no written reference to it that I could find - nothing in the dictionary, the encyclopedia, the card catalogue, books in print or anywhere else I looked. I called the lady who did the reading for me. She said, "You know I'm in an altered state when I do readings. I have no idea what 'Reiki' is." "Well," I figured, "I either hallucinated this word, or I'm spelling it wrong. Either way, I'll just have to forget it for now." So I did.

My cousin Kathy used to work with me, and she would joke that I had "Sucker" tattooed on my forehead in some kind of invisible ink or secret code, because anyone who came into the shop and requested a donation was pretty sure of getting one. I always thought it was good karma. A representative from the local Waldorf school came in one day, wanting shops to donate goods or services for them to sell at a fund raising auction, to bring their rent current yet again.

I've always thought the Waldorf schools are the next best thing to sliced bread, and was very willing to help them. However, I did ask one thing. "The last time I had donated service for an auction to set up a day care center, $100 worth of service sold for only five bucks because almost no one came to the auction. So can I come to this auction to buy back this service, at a reasonable rate, of course, if only a few people show up? That way you'll at least get some money." "Can you come? Of course you can come! Can you bring any solvent friends with you?"

That sounded like a great thing to do, so I began calling some of my more solvent friends, and explained that they should bring money, we were going to support this wonderful school. I gathered a fair number, and we all got dressed up to go to the auction. It was held at one of the restored turn of the century hotels, and promised to be a good time.

There were a lot of people there. And a lot of things for auction. Obviously the school had been busy. Offered for bids among the pony rides, 100 gallons of gasoline, catered dinner for eight, clowns for a birthday party and other wonderful assorted things, was a *Reiki* treatment. It was clear that at least a few other people had heard the word, the competition was fairly brisk, but I finally bought the treatment just to find out what this "Reiki" was.

I made an appointment with the woman offering the treatment. Her name was Marti Pease, and she was a teacher at the Waldorf school. She was a first level practitioner at the time. Soft spoken and kindly appearing she stood at about the level of my shoulder. It was evening, after work for me. She invited me in, showed me into a small living room that doubled as a treatment room. The incense was burning, the lights were low, the music was playing, and there was a day bed in the center of the room. Marti asked me to "make myself comfortable" and lie down on the bed.

I had no idea what she meant by that statement, so I came right to the point and asked her. "Make myself comfortable. Do you mean get naked, as in a massage?"

"Oh, my God, no!" she said, looking up at me, fairly shocked. "Don't do THAT!"

So, I said, "Well, you need to tell me what this is all about, because I don't have a clue as to what 'Reiki' is."

She said that she couldn't actually tell me, but she could show me, if I would kindly lie down, with all my clothes on. Which I did.

She covered me with a blanket, and then sat at my head and put her hands over my eyes. And I couldn't breathe. "This is curious," I thought, between the measured breaths I was taking to keep from hyperventilating. "I wonder if this is supposed to be relaxing. Breathe! If it is, I wonder when the relaxing part kicks in? Breathe!"

The relaxation part did kick in after a few more positions, somewhere on my chest. My breathing evened out on its own, my body relaxed, and I felt like I dozed off and on. I don't remember much more about the treatment except for some really vibrant colors that I saw in my head occasionally.

I have always been an avowed alternative-therapy-workshop junkie, so I was at least familiar with different forms and feelings of energy work.

At that point of my life I had also spent a number of years working with psychic healing techniques. The one thing I knew about this treatment was that what ever this woman was doing, it was real.

I could feel the energy flowing from her hands through my body, and feel the physiological effects that energy was having. And she didn't seem to be doing a lot to produce the effects - not much preparation that I could see, no chanting, no special robes, no turning around three times and spitting over her left shoulder - just hands on. I was impressed.

After the treatment we talked a bit about my experience. We figured that the work I did as a hairdresser, holding my arms above heart level for most of the day, had traumatized my upper body muscles. When these muscles experienced this "relaxing" Reiki energy for the first time, they simply seized up. That's why I had trouble breathing, not to mention the amount of hair spray and chemicals I inhaled each day. I'm happy to report that after a number of sessions of Reiki, my body got through or past that initial reaction, and I could feel the peaceful relaxing energy right away.

In the years since that first treatment, I have given and received a lot of Reiki. My first experience is not common. Most people feel relaxed, and often fall into a light sleep or a meditative state by about the third head position. I share my experience with you to let you know that a Reiki treatment is not always peaceful and calm, restful and relaxing all the way through. Sometimes change is uncomfortable for a while. Yet, Reiki is always, consistently wonderful, and is always used by the body to move toward health and balance, and there can be a few bumps along the way.

So I asked Marti Pease how I could learn more about this Reiki, perhaps even learn how to do it myself. She said that I had to go to a Master to learn, attend a training and become initiated. Nothing was written about Reiki because it was an oral tradition, and not something that could be passed on or learned about in books. It had taken me three months to find a definition for the word! Hearing that I had to find a Master to learn more about this wasn't great news. "A Master. Wonderful. Where does one find one of *those*? Tibet?"

Marti said that, actually, she would be sponsoring a Reiki Master (the only one on the East coast at that time) to teach a level one class in the area in a few months. Would I be interested in attending that class? (In Burnt Hills, New York. About as big as it sounds.)

I was surely interested. When would it be? In the spring, a Friday night, all day Saturday, and Sunday morning. (Take a weekend off from work? Unheard of. I'm self employed, no work no pay, and weekends are my biggest money.) How much would it be? (If it's cheap I can justify the time off.) "$125." (At that time) "What? For a weekend?" (Way too expensive - that was of a week's worth of groceries!)

Then I thought if I could spend that amount at the grocery store without batting an eye, I could surely come up with an equivalent amount by the time spring came.

Marti just sat there quietly, not encouraging me, and waited for me to make up my mind. No sales pitch, no prompting. She simply let the Reiki, the treatment, speak for itself. I was either called to take this class or not.

I was called. I signed up. An avowed workaholic at the time, I took the time off from work, and found that the world didn't stop turning. The Reiki class turned out to be the best investment I have ever made with time or money. It quite simply changed my life.

The Reiki level I training began on a Friday night. I got my first glimpse of Linda Keiser, (now Keiser Mardis), the Teaching Master, standing near the door. She had a glow about her that was not from $50 facials - I knew what $50 facials looked like, what they did for a person, and this was beyond that. This looked and felt more like the energy around one who meditates a lot. I decided that what ever it was that she had, I wanted to know how to find that for myself.

Linda sat in the circle of introductions, talked about the history of Reiki and shared some things about her personal path. Then we each received an initiation, the first of four during the class - sort of an attunement to this healing energy. We sat in a circle sharing Reiki while this went on. When the person behind me came back from their initiation, completing the circle, it was like a current of energy went through all of us. I remember a very clear thought passing through my mind at that moment - that this feeling of Reiki was the most comforting thing I had ever felt in my life.

It seemed like another current of energy came around, and with this came another very clear thought: I couldn't do anything better with my life than to share this feeling with other people - that a person could experience such comfort just by placing hands on yourself or another! Astounding!

My next thought brought me back to the real world, ("Will you get real, honey?") reminding me that I had a family to raise (six sons, five teenagers and a pre-teen at that time), a business to run, a marriage to attend to (with a husband who did not share my metaphysical interests, to put it mildly), animals to feed (two dogs, three cats and a tank full of tropical fish), and what was I thinking anyway? I promised my conscious mind that I would not get carried away if it would just shut up and let me enjoy the weekend. It was agreed.

However, those two very clear thoughts stayed with me all weekend. By the time the class was over and we were leaving, I had worked up the nerve to ask Linda how I could go further in Reiki. I knew I had found something wonderful and I didn't want to let it go.

Linda told me there were only three levels of training in the Usui System, and that I never actually needed to go any further at all. The first level had everything I would need to know for my own practice. The second level of Reiki dealt with conscious use of the energy, and if I wanted to pursue it I would be eligible in the summer after practicing the first level for a minimum of 100 days. The cost was $500.

That was a bit beyond the equivalent of grocery money. Such a substantial amount of money was certainly not something I could come up with at a moment's notice. I decided to turn it over to the Universe. There is a saying that Great Spirit knows your rent, knows what you need to show up and do your right work in the world. So I put it out to the Universe that if I were meant to go on to this next level, that I would get the $500, outside of my budget. (I was very clear about that point).

It came. I went.

How the money came, and how I made my decision to go to the next training is too long a story for right here and now, I'll tell it another time. Most of it is woven into this book.

I did take my next level of training with Linda in August of 1985. The class was large and spread over two days. During this time I had a dream that I was to become a Teaching Master. Shortly after the class, I wrote to Linda to tell her of all the experiences I had had practicing Reiki between my first and second level training. These seemed like normal life at the time, yet were some of the most important experiences of my life. I told her I knew I was supposed to do more with Reiki, pursue the Master path so I could teach, although I had no idea of what was involved with that, or how I would accomplish it. It would seem I was busy enough without taking on anything else. I just knew I had to go further with Reiki.

Linda wrote back and explained what my commitments in the Master path would be. When she got to the financial commitment, ($10,000.00 - *how* many zeros is that?) I decided to talk to the Universe again. I came to understand that if this was truly my path, the ways and means would be provided. My job was to recognize and acknowledge my truth, trust in it, and simply take the next steps.

The next steps in this case were to begin attending Reiki I and II trainings with Linda. This is an oral tradition and this is how it is passed on - I would sit in enough classes that I would learn how to teach by absorption. This workaholic started taking weekends off to attend classes, at least the ones in New England. And I began sponsoring classes in Saratoga Springs. My training began. My practice began. I incorporated Reiki into my life.

Linda guided my Master candidacy training for the next three years. Mastery in the Usui System of Natural Healing requires preparation, practice and commitment far beyond anything I have ever encountered, other than parenthood. The story of those years of preparation and training can also be told another time.

Linda Keiser Mardis initiated me as a Teaching Master in the Usui System of Natural Healing in April 1988. I have never looked back.

It is truly the best thing I can do with my life, to share this gift of Reiki with others. I have practiced and taught Reiki almost all the way around the world. I'm only missing the space between Nepal and Indonesia - I traveled east on one trip and west on the other. I expect to fill that in sometime soon. This path has been consistently wonderful, and more than I could have ever imagined. As we say in Reiki - Thank you, all my students, for allowing me to be your teacher, and thank you especially for teaching me.

Namaste!

Penelope Jewell
November, 1995

REIKI - UNIVERSAL LIFE ENERGY

What Reiki Is:

Reiki is a Japanese word representing Universal Life Energy, which is the energy that is all around us. It also represents the Universal Life Force (Rei) brought through personal energy (Ki) for the purposes of balance and healing, as in the Usui System of Natural Healing. Hawayo Takata (the woman who brought Reiki out of Japan) called it God-power. I think of Reiki as the divine within - that force or energy which makes us alive as opposed to dead - innately connected to the greater, infinite divine energy which surrounds us. This energy *is* the life force, the quickening in each cell, it is that which creates and supports life; positive, healing and balancing in nature.

This energy which surrounds us is a lot like the air that we breathe. We don't often think about being surrounded by energy just as we are surrounded by air, and yet we are. We don't usually notice the air we breathe unless there is a change or disturbance in it - if it is "stuffy" or fresh, if there is a breeze, or a perfume, or pollution. We can feel differences in energy the same way - notice the energy of being in a cathedral, at a party, in a room where a baby is sleeping, or where an argument has recently occurred.

Just as oxygen can be extracted from air and given to a person who needs it to support their healing; there is a healing, balancing band or vibration in the energy which surrounds us that can be extracted (or concentrated) and offered to a person in the same way. Some people have a natural gift for this, and some people learn how to do this in a conscious way - such as moving chi or energy in the martial arts for the purpose of healing injuries, or taking a training in Reiki.

It is the initiations or attunements in the Usui System of Natural Healing - Reiki that allow us to be the filter for this energy, to transmit healing energy to ourselves or whatever we touch. This requires no conscious technique or knowledge - simply practice - putting hands on for treatment of self or others. Anyone can learn how to do this. My personal theory is that we all have this ability, talent or gift - an innate knowing of how to consciously bring healing energy through our bodies. We simply have forgotten how to use it on a daily basis. Actually I don't think we would have survived as a species if we didn't understand how to use our energy for healing ourselves. Reiki is a direct reconnection to, or reawakening of, this innate body knowledge.

History and Elements of the Form of the Usui System of Natural Healing - Reiki

In your Reiki I class you may hear the entire story of Dr. Mikao Usui, Dr. Chujiro Hayashi, and Mrs. Hawayo Takata. Telling the story, sharing the history in an oral tradition, is part of the form of the Usui System, and a very important part of any class I teach.

There is an energetic transmission that happens between a Master and a student when a Master tells the story. It is the difference between reading a play, or being present as prepared and gifted players perform a play. There is something beyond the words, beyond the transfer of information, that takes place. It is about being touched, about receiving something more than can be explained with words alone.

So, I won't recount the story with all its details here. There are written stories about Mikao Usui's journey in some of the books listed in the "Recommended Reading" section in the back if you would like to read about it. I hope you have the experience of hearing the story "live". I have heard it, and told it, many times and it still holds my interest.

For now, let us just say that a man named Mikao Usui, sometime in the late 1800's, went on a journey to find the answer to a question: "How does physical healing occur?" His quest to find the answer took him many places, from being a teacher to being a student, a monk, a healer, and back to a being a teacher again - teaching people one at a time how to heal themselves and each other. His vision was so clear and strong that it has enabled the answer he found to be passed on from himself to millions of practitioners today.

Chujiro Hayashi was one of the Masters initiated by Mikao Usui. Hayashi opened a healing center in Tokyo in the early 1900's, where he trained many practitioners. He may have been the first to collect clinical evidence about the practice of the Usui System. Chujiro Hayashi initiated thirteen Masters, including Hawayo Takata, a first generation Japanese-American woman who came to his clinic for treatment in the early 1930s. Mrs. Takata stayed on at the clinic to study the practice of the Usui System, and subsequently brought Reiki out of Japan to Hawaii before the second World War. She was initiated as a Master by Hayashi February 21, 1938, Mrs. Takata trained and initiated twenty two teaching Masters, and taught classes in the Usui System of Natural Healing - Reiki until her death in 1980.

The Usui System of Natural Healing has been taught through an oral tradition since its inception, meaning that a practitioner learns the system, in person and hands-on, from a trained teaching Master. This system cannot be learned or passed on through the written word. It is an experience, not an intellectual exercise.

Elements Of The Form Of The Usui System Of Natural Healing - Reiki

Precepts: there are five Reiki healing precepts or principles. These concepts are meant to be incorporated into daily life. You saw them listed in slightly different forms at the front of this book. Japanese is a picture language, so there are often different translations into words. This is a translation from Usui's notes.

The Five Precepts

Today, feel no anger.
Have no worries.
Feel gratitude.
Show diligence in your undertakings.
Treat others with kindness.

Treatments: formal treatments follow a prescribed form: three sections, four positions in each section, approximately five minutes of Reiki in each position.

Symbols: three symbols are given in the second degree.

Initiations: there are four separate initiations in the first level of Reiki training, one initiation in the second level, and one initiation for Master level.

Oral tradition: there is a relationship with a Master in order to learn the system.

Form of teaching: four sections over a two to four day period for a first level class. There is a minimum of 100 days practice between Reiki I and II; a suggested minimum of three years practice and training between Reiki I and Mastery; and a suggested minimum of five to six years teaching/practice before considering training another Master, if the Master feels called to take on that responsibility.

History: the story of Reiki is shared at each first level class.

Money: is a part of the form, and signifies commitment along with time, energy, and practice. Prices can vary, depending upon the country and sometimes the circumstances, according to the individual discretion of the Teaching Master. First level Reiki training fee is $150 - $250, second level is $500, Master fee is $10,000. Energy exchange means an exchange commensurate with the monetary fee.

This outline is a general agreement of the elements of the form of the Usui System of Natural Healing - Reiki by the Masters who practice it. There are exceptions.

Each Master within the Usui System endeavors to practice and teach within the form of the System, as it was given to them, without any changes or additions. And each Master is also a unique expression of this energy, an individual embodiment of the form, and responsible to their own inner knowing in their practice and teaching.

Form of Reiki Classes or Trainings

Reiki level I classes are usually held in four consecutive two to three hour sessions, over a period of two to four days. This allows time for integration of both the attunements and of the idea that normal people can use energy for healing purposes.

The usual content of the class is:

Section one: introductions, story of Reiki, first attunement, self healing positions.

Section two: demonstration of head positions by Master, including some discussion of physical components of each position; second attunement; practice by students.

Section three: demonstrate chest positions, discussion, third attunement, practice.

Section four: demonstrate back positions, discussion, fourth attunement, practice, closing.

The form of a Reiki level II class is somewhat different. Level II is taught only after the student has practiced level I for at least 100 days. Again, this allows for assimilation of the energy, and gives time for the student to incorporate the physical practice of Reiki into their lives, giving a basis of balance and support.

Reiki is primarily a tool for self healing. It requires hands-on practice, it does not work in theory. It only works if you actually use it. Even professional practitioners and Masters use Reiki for themselves first, self healing on a daily basis, and then sharing with others.

There are only three levels in the Usui System. The third level is called Master, and encompasses a way of life: practicing the system personally as well as professionally. This includes self treatment and incorporating the principles in daily life; giving treatment to others, maintaining a practice; teaching classes; and when called, training and initiating Masters within the form of the Usui System. I like the Japanese phrase that describes this level - do shu - where a way is practiced. Mastery is lived, not attained; a way of life, not a destination; a path, not a goal; a commitment, not a credential.

Attunement to the Energy

Through four initiations, or energy attunements in the first level class, we become capable of conveying or transferring Reiki, which is the healing, balancing band or vibration of energy in the ocean of energy which surrounds us.

In class, I explain this process by using the cookie press, cookie dough theory. I hope you have seen a cookie press work. There is a template at the bottom of the press that filters the dough and determines the shape of the cookies. So, as long as there is dough in the press, we can poop out, say, Christmas tree shaped cookies by the dozens. When we get tired of trees, we can change the template and make wreaths instead.

The initiations are like putting a template - a thought form or idea - in our consciousness that says, "Only healing, balancing energy passes through here from now on." We could create this template within our consciousness to filter healing energy. In other kinds of healing we would do this with our thoughts, concentration, preparations, and intentions to heal. With Reiki this template process is automatic, and always there, through the four initiations or attunements which are part of the first level of the Usui System.

The initiations are consecutive and cumulative, you need all four to have Reiki "work". It is like dialing a telephone number, if you don't use all the numbers in the right sequence, you won't be connected where you want to be. The initiations are performed by a trained and initiated Reiki Master. Once you have these initiations you have the capability of using Reiki forever, as long as you keep using it, at least a few minutes a day.

There is actually nothing to "learn" in a Reiki class, although there are things to practice. The initiations remind you of your innate connection to divine energy, remind you how to use it, strengthen and deepen that connection, and clear it of any energetic debris. One of my teachers explained it like gutters and downspouts: on a newly constructed house, the gutters and downspouts are free and clear. The rain falls, rolls down the roof, collects in the gutter and whooshes down to the ground. Ten or fifteen years later, if the gutters and downspouts have not been cleaned, the rain rolls down the roof, soaks into the dead leaves, pine needles and squirrels' nests, and barely trickles to the ground.

Our energy centers and systems in our body are something like those gutters and downspouts. When we are newborn, our energetic gutters and downspouts are all in place: clean, clear and in working order. Our energy flows freely. We are clearly connected to our source of energy, and use it without thinking about it.

As we get older and more socialized, and cultureized, we can consciously cut down on our ability to use energy - especially if we believe that because we can't actually see it, it doesn't work or even exist. We (hopefully) can't see air, either, and we breathe just fine. What the initiations do, basically, is blow the crap out of our energetic gutters and downspouts so energy flows freely again. Our use of Reiki keeps the passageways clear and clean. The more we practice Reiki, on ourselves and/or others, the greater our capacity to share Reiki. If we don't use it, we tend to lose it - our capacity diminishes.

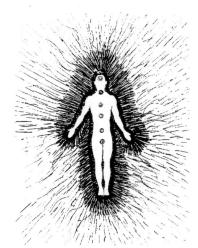

Our energetic passageways are called chakras in some traditions. Chakra means spinning wheel or vortex. I explain chakras like this: We have physical energetic centers: our eyes take in impulses that translate to sight, our ears take in sound waves that translate to hearing, our noses take in odors through the air, mouths take in physical sustenance in liquid and solid form. Each intake of energy is in denser or finer form - some so fine we can only measure it by result - like sight. Our energetic centers or chakras are like that - each takes in its own vibrational level of energy for different uses.

There are many books that give a fuller explanation of chakras and their functions. I'll just give you an overview here. Basically, we have seven major chakras within the body. The crown chakra (seventh, top of the head, deals with the spiritual vibration of energy) points straight up to the sky, the base chakra (first, base of the spine, between the legs, deals with the life force energy) points down to the earth.

The rest of the chakras are aligned in front of the spine, in the center of the body, and open front and back. The second or Ki chakra is about three inches below the navel and is the center of gravity for your body. It deals with feelings, is often called the passion chakra, but don't confuse this with sex, it is simply how you feel about being alive - self esteem at a very basic level. The third chakra is the solar plexus, and deals with universal healing - you don't have to deserve it, you just have to accept it. Same for the fourth or heart chakra - universal love, as much as you are willing to receive. The fifth or throat chakra deals with communication, both internal (thoughts manifested as feelings, feelings interpreted into visual/verbal thoughts) and external communication. If your internal communication is clear, you at least have a shot at your external communication being clear. The sixth chakra is in the center of your forehead, the third eye or pineal gland, and deals with your perceptions, including extra sensory. Each chakra has a particular vibration, color and sound or tone associated with it.

REIKI ENERGY

What Reiki Does (and Doesn't):

Reiki brings balance and healing to the body, mind and spirit. It accelerates the body's natural ability to heal itself, while opening the mind and spirit to causes of disease, disharmony and pain. Reiki is a support to the body, and therefore works in conjunction with and as an adjunct to other forms of treatment and therapy. In reestablishing balance, Reiki helps the body to cleanse itself of toxins. Reiki works on any living thing - anything with an energy field - including plants, animals and people. And you do not have to be ill to enjoy the benefits of a Reiki treatment. Healthy bodies often experience an enhanced feeling of peace and well being.

The flow and use of the Reiki energy is determined by the recipient's body, which draws the energy through the practitioner's body. Reiki cannot be directed by the practitioner, or by the consciousness of the recipient, or by the opinion of anyone else. This is why you can't do Reiki wrong. The recipient's body receives this energy, and the recipient's body uses the energy for its highest good. The body has an innate wisdom far greater than any logic, intellectual process, desire or understanding any of us may have. I like this about Reiki - I can't direct its use in any body, therefore I can't misuse it in any way, or even inadvertently screw it up.

That is also why the results of a Reiki treatment cannot be predicted. If you and I and your Aunt Fanny think that the pain of your bursitis should be relieved, that is all very well and good. Perhaps your body knows that first your liver needs help using the medication you are taking, and the bursitis pain remains at the same level it was when you came in. Perhaps it would take several more treatments for your body to come to the balance needed to release some or all of the pain. Sometimes the body responds by relaxing and releasing pain immediately. Neither you nor I nor your Aunt Fanny can change the way your body uses this energy - thank God.

As a practitioner, we treat the body, not the disease; the person, not the problem. When the body is in balance healing can occur, and Reiki gently brings the body to balance, helping it maintain that balance longer with each treatment. So, we give full treatments as often as possible. Acute conditions often respond quickly, chronic conditions often require a series of treatments. As practitioners we do not need to know the presenting problem even if there is one, and we do not need to look for any cause and effect, Reiki balances both. And of course as a Reiki practitioner we do not diagnose or prescribe, that is none of our business, out of our depth, and illegal for very good reasons. Reiki itself is simple, and profoundly effective.

Allowing Reiki to Work

I think of Reiki as activating and supporting the divine or life force energy within myself or another. That activation brings healing to all aspects of a person, whether we see it or not. This energy within each cell of the body, the living part of the body/mind/spirit, has a wisdom far greater than any information I may have stored in my head. That is why I don't get to direct the healing energy to any place or situation with a result in mind. That is why I cannot promise any particular change from a treatment. There will be change in a positive direction, for sure. I just don't get to predict what it will look like, or how great it will be, or when it will happen. This may be a blow to my ego. I'll get over it.

There may be no obvious physical changes that we can observe with our gross senses, especially in one treatment. A person in pain from arthritis may come for a treatment, and may go home again in pain from arthritis. However, that person may be more at peace with themselves, kinder to those around them for the next few days. Perhaps they sleep more comfortably, or their appetite improves. Their attitude may have needed, and received, the healing. These changes may be subtle, but they are powerful. The general direction is always one of healing and balancing.

Consistency is a Key

If treatments are given and received consistently, enormous changes can and do occur. It is possible that in some cases we actually prepare our bodies for dis-ease through non-supportive conditions, behaviors or attitudes in our life. If this is so, we can prepare our bodies for health, too. Reiki brings the body gently back to balance with each treatment, each time the balance lasts a little longer and supports more healing.

In this balanced place we may find less need for some of our non-supportive behaviors, attitudes, habits or even addictions. Releasing the need for a behavior or a substance can allow us to release the conditions produced by them. Reiki naturally fills those spaces with healing energy, so we don't produce those conditions again out of familiarity or habit. We become used to our new, balanced place of health and well being, and become interested in maintaining it.

The practice of Reiki is cumulative. With daily treatments, often even a degenerative condition can reverse - stop degenerating, come to a balance, and begin to generate healthy tissue or conditions again. Sometimes healing is found in letting go of the body and making a peaceful transition. Reiki supports healing in all categories and conditions.

Unless a person is simply coming to experience a treatment for the experience of it, four treatments in a row is usually a good way for a person to start working on a condition in their body or even in their lives. Things didn't get out of alignment overnight, and probably won't get back in alignment overnight either, although that can happen. I always like to allow for miracles. Most of the time we have to emotionally prepare ourselves to accept changes in our body/mind/spirit entity, even good ones.

In general, Reiki works quickly and visibly on acute conditions, and for general balance in chronic conditions. The body may be balancing itself for a long time before we see any visible results, and then it just seems that it happened overnight. In general, symptoms will disappear in the reverse order of their occurrence - the most recently acquired symptom will be the first symptom to leave.

If I am working with someone with emphysema or arthritis or any degenerative or auto-immune disease I ask the person to allow for about thirty consecutive treatments, at least two and better three treatments a week. At some point I also expect them to do something to support their own healing in addition to the treatments, and in addition to any physician's care they may receive. This might take the form of taking a Reiki course themselves, doing therapy, counseling or even affirmations.

If they have any detrimental habits like smoking, I ask them to make some move toward giving these habits up, and remind them that the Reiki itself will support that effort. Reiki treatments actually help the body release the physical craving for substances like tobacco, alcohol, or sugar, and can help balance emotional needs that may underlie these habits.

Occasionally, conditions may get worse before they get better. It sometimes happens that way. No, you didn't do anything wrong. Remember, you can't do Reiki wrong. Actually, you didn't even do anything, Reiki did. Reiki catalyzes the body's natural ability to heal itself. This is a good news/bad news sort of situation. Sometimes by speeding up the healing, things look or feel worse for a while. The good news is, they get over faster. Feeling worse is especially true in burns and abrasions - they tend to hurt more, just like a burn feels hotter when you run warm water over it.

Remember first aid for most burns is immediate cold water, while you think about whether or not you want to do Reiki. If you do decide to give Reiki, you may want to keep your hands above the physical body, in the energy field. Don't touch the affected area directly even if it is covered with a sterile dressing . It may be painful for the recipient.

I once spilled an entire pan of boiling water over my hand. I didn't realize the lid was loose. As soon as I could get to the sink I drew a basin of cold water, and submerged my burned hand, with my other hand on top, giving Reiki. I knew the burn was severe and would probably require further attention, I just wanted to get the pain under control before I went to the emergency room. It took about half an hour to calm down. When I finally took my hand out of the water there were no blisters, so I did more Reiki. Within the hour there was no evidence that I had received such a burn.

Support

Sometimes I work with people who have a chronic condition or disease. I find that it is important for people to support their own healing. I always suggest that they learn Reiki for themselves, and give themselves daily treatment to support whatever else is going on, whatever other therapies are being used, including whatever treatments I may be giving them. We talk about positive attitudes and affirmations, nourishing the self on all levels, willingness to release the disease, and willingness to accept good health with all its blessings and responsibilities.

Sometimes it is necessary for the person to acknowledge the benefits of being ill before they can really become well. A person receiving more attention, assistance, or money, for being unwell may be subconsciously reluctant to actually get well, and may put it off as long as possible. These are real considerations, not judgments. When looked at consciously, at least there is a chance this situation can be changed, if the person so desires. They actually may not want to get well. And this is where you get to practice honoring another person's path, even if you don't agree with it. You don't have to like it. You do have to honor it.

As a caregiver, I have often felt blessed to have this gift of Reiki. Even if I am not giving a formal treatment, I can give Reiki just by holding a person's hand as I sit beside them. If I am caring for someone ill or in pain, especially chronic or long term, Reiki helps me keep my energy and spirits up, a very important thing.

Integrity of the System

The integrity of the Usui System of Natural Healing lies first in the ability of the recipient to accept or reject the energy. If accepted, the recipient's body uses the energy for its highest good at that moment, as the divine intelligence and innate inner wisdom of that person directs it. Not where their intellect, or their mother's intellect, or my intellect may think the energy needs to go, but where the body's own wisdom directs it. In the same way, their healing doesn't happen how they, or their mother, or I think it should, except coincidentally.

This relieves me of an enormous responsibility. I don't have to know anything, or do anything other than Reiki. I simply have to place hands on the body, my own or another, and let Reiki do the work. Reiki will activate the divine within, go where it is needed and support the body to do whatever is needed. The only assistance required is my willingness to do the treatment. Reiki is enough.

So the essence of Reiki for me is empowerment of the individual, at every level. When I receive a treatment, my body/mind/spirit receives the energy and is empowered to heal itself. When I take the first level training, I am empowered to give Reiki to myself and others, and again the energy is used as each individual body/mind/spirit directs. At the second level, I am empowered to use Reiki in the more metaphysical realms, beyond physical touch, and still each recipient uses the energy for themselves. At no point here is any belief required of me, nor do I have to subscribe to any dogma. I only have to practice in the form I was taught, basically, "This is a hand, this is a body, this is Reiki. Use it."

I don't need to be in a state of grace to give or receive Reiki, either. Actually, I can even be feeling quite cranky (who, me?) and within a few positions the Reiki itself will bring relaxation and a peaceful feeling. I don't have to know my right hand from my left hand; or take my jewelry off (unless it is noisy, painful, or intrusive like that beeper watch that goes off in my ear); or do mighty preparations, like turn around three times and spit over my left shoulder. I just lay hands on and it works.

Healing and Curing

There is a difference between healing and curing, although they can be concurrent. Healing means to come to balance. An imbalance in physical or emotional health, exhibited by disharmony or dis-ease, can dissolve and/or disappear as the body regains its natural, healthy balance. It is in balance that healing occurs. That is all any medicine or therapy is ever meant to do - bring the body back to balance so natural healing can occur. Support Mother Nature. Let Nature take its course.

Curing means to "get rid of (an ailment or a problem)": to affect a change back to where the problem did not exist. Curing is often pursued without understanding or dealing with the cause(s) of the dis-ease or imbalance. Ultimately, unless the cause is treated, on purpose or by accident, the imbalance may reoccur. Reiki addresses all levels of an imbalance without our having to know what that imbalance is, where it began or what it may be affecting in the physical, mental, emotional, spiritual realms. Each body's natural wisdom uses the energy where and as it is needed.

Healing may be more subtle than a cure. And measurability is a factor in the Western world. The effects of Reiki are individual, therefore not consistently predictable, and may not show up in obvious places. So the scientific community often finds it difficult to devise tests comprehensive enough to measure "real" results. Results must also be measurable in mathematical language, or they don't exist in "scientific" terms. Recipients not used to subjective support may confuse subtle with ineffective. The subtle, the subjective and the experiential sometimes have a difficult time proving themselves real in mathematical language, but they do exist, and they do make an enormous difference in the quality of life.

I admit to my share of wanting Reiki to work in ways I thought it should: in measurable ways, to prove how great it is; and on my time line - right now - to relieve symptoms or pain so the person could get back to their normal or usual level of functioning as soon as possible. Luckily, none of my wants make a pinch of difference in how Reiki works. I admit to learning about letting go, and letting Reiki work. I am not the "healer". Neither are you. We are just the channels for healing energy. The recipient is the one who does the healing.

Through my own practice and experience, I continue to learn about patience, about being willing to allow healing to happen on the body's own time line, for that body's highest good. I continue to learn about honoring the healing process and path of another, whatever that process may be. I don't have to like it or agree with it, I do have to honor it. I believe there is a higher wisdom at work than my own. I believe there is a bigger pattern being woven than I can see from where I stand.

My personal belief system allows that I had some choice in the path I would walk this time around before I ever came in this world. Perhaps I chose my general circumstances before I came in for the opportunities these circumstances would allow me and those travelling with me. My soul's development may require some particular handicap or disease, at some particular time in my life, possibly from inception, even though I may not consciously understand the purposes served by this. It might not be the finest thing a well meaning person could do for me - to "cure" me – to take those circumstances away, so that I do not have to live, learn, and/or grow through them. "Perfect" is not necessarily "right", "imperfect" is not necessarily "wrong". Healing – acceptance, coming to peace, balance, and harmony with a life situation - healing is a different matter.

Other Types of Healing

The recipient's body decides to accept, then determines the flow and use of the Reiki energy being offered. This feature of the recipient's body determining use makes Reiki unique in my experience - unlike any other form of healing that I have encountered.

Western medicine, physical medical healing, has three recognized forms: *allopathy, osteopathy, and homeopathy*, all of which are physical and invasive to one degree or another. Metaphysical healing has three forms most often mentioned: *faith, psychic and spiritual*. All of these are meta-physical - beyond the physical, and non-invasive on the physical level. On an intervention scale of one to ten, Reiki is a one and surgery is a ten.

In the Western, physical/medical healing world:

Allopathy is the most common form of medical healing and is done by an MD - medical doctor. It uses drugs and/or surgery, very occasionally diet or attitude, to induce a condition different from the cause of the disease/dysfunction in the body.

Osteopathy is done by a DO - doctor of osteopathy, or osteopath. Osteopathy uses less intervention by drugs or surgery, and depends more upon manipulation of the body bones, tissue or muscles to produce a desired change.

Homeopathy, practiced by RSc. or D. Hom, or homeopaths, is a method which induces change in a condition by using minute amounts of a drug that would produce symptoms similar to those being exhibited by the person being treated.

In the metaphysical healing world:

In **psychic healing**, a practitioner directs healing energy to a particular area of a body with their mind or spirit, usually with a particular result in mind.

 In **faith healing**, either the practitioner or the recipient, or both, must have a belief or faith that the practitioner has a gift for healing; or is a channel for some greater power/deity that has an ability to bring about healing in that body.

Some **spiritual healing** is closer to faith healing, channeling divine energy; and some spiritual healing is more in the category of channeling entities – disincarnate angels, spirits or guides.

The spiritual healer has a belief or faith that s/he is the vehicle for, can channel, facilitate or direct divine energy and/or a spirit/s, (a disincarnate personal energy form) who has the ability to heal or facilitate healing in another. S/he trusts that the spirit knows what it is doing, and has the body's higher good in mind as it does its work.

In contrast to psychic healing, Reiki energy is not directed by the practitioner. In Reiki, the recipient's body/spirit accepts the flow of healing energy, determines where it is needed and how it is used. No conscious direction is used by either party. This empowerment of the individual is part of the integrity of the system from receiving a treatment through the first, second and Master levels of practice.

In contrast to faith healing or spiritual healing, Reiki is belief free. Neither party has to believe anything about Reiki. "Hands on - Reiki on, hands off - Reiki off," Takata would say to her students. Reiki is a simple (albeit profound) energy technique. When your hands are on the body, Reiki energy is available. Reiki works automatically, not because the giver or receiver believed something, did something right, or had a "gift". In fact, you can't do Reiki wrong. Isn't that a relief?

While we are explaining what Reiki isn't, Reiki is not a religion. Reiki is about personal practice and experience. There is no dogma, there is nothing to believe except your own experience. The elements of the form of the Usui System of Natural Healing that you will find listed earlier, including the five Reiki Healing Principles or Precepts are simply verbal explanations of the concepts found in the form of the Usui System of Natural Healing - Reiki. These concepts are simply so. Whether or not you believe them, or believe in them, does not alter their reality, or affect your practice.

Just as there is nothing to believe, there is really nothing to learn beyond the hand positions, and even those adjust to particular bodies and circumstances. Once you have been initiated into Reiki, the rest is up to you and your personal application of practice with yourself and others. Reiki is practice in its essence.

As I say in the beginning of my classes, most of what will be talked about is merely entertainment for the left brain, the side that likes data and information; while the right brain (the side that understands concepts and thinks in three dimensions) gets on with actually practicing this wonderful healing art. And practice is the key - you don't have to be an expert, as a matter of fact, I really don't know any Reiki experts. I only know some people who practice a lot, some enough to be considered professional, some who make it a way of life. Maybe this is a little like golf and sex - two other things you don't have to be good at to enjoy, as they say.

ENERGETICS 101

More About Energy and Treatments

Good Vibrations

We are energy bodies. I know we think we are solid. But we think the earth is solid, too, and trees and grass and plants grow out of it, so it can't be all that solid. Well, neither are we. We are made up of atoms, and atoms are mostly space. If the nucleus of an atom were at the bottom left hand corner of this page, the first electron would be at the top right hand corner. That is a lot of empty space.

What holds the atom together is centrifugal force - energy vibration. So each atom, its structure determined by its own substance pattern, number of electrons, etc., has its own particular vibration. Imagine that the vibration is perceivable - like a musical tone or even a color.

Did you ever play with a yo-yo when you were a kid? And when you got tired of yo-yo-ing, you swung the yo-yo around your head? Remember how the string looked like a white blur and there was a sound that changed according to how fast you swung the yo-yo? That helps me imagine the color/sound vibration of an atom.

Atoms come together to form molecules, multiplying exponentially the possibilities of the expression of life. As they come together, it is like individual instruments forming a band, or voices in a chorus, or primary colors being mixed to form subtle variations. The vibrations blend to form new, more complex vibrations. If these vibrations had a pitch I would imagine it to become lower and fuller with each combination. If these vibrations were color, I would imagine that color to be denser.

As the molecules come together, they eventually form substances, cells, tissues, then the organs and systems of the body - each with their own particular vibration. You could imagine your liver having its own energetic/vibrational aura – its own color and tone quality; your spleen a different vibrational tone (color and sound), and so on with all your "instruments". So, on a good day, you are like a symphony orchestra – each individual instrument making its own clear sound and the combination producing magnificent vibrations that are in tune with each other and in harmony with the Universe. The body really is electric and really does sing, it really is made up of energy.

Emotional Physiology

Speaking about tones and vibrations, emotions are vibrational, too. Love and anger can both be red hot, but they are certainly not the same, and don't feel the same. They both register in the body, though, and we feel the physiological effects and reactions. Why do we feel emotions in different places? Why do we get a physiological reaction that makes us open our heart, smile, laugh, shed tears, feel our stomach tighten, blood rise, hair stand on end?

There is a theory (#53 if you are counting) that emotions can match the energetic vibrations of the organs and glands in our body, and can register or even remain as energetic impressions with that organ or gland. For instance, shock and trauma register with the adrenals, and may remain as an energetic memory there. Doing Reiki on the adrenals can actually release or heal a memory held there.

So it is not really the wrinkles in the brain that record all our experiences, as I always thought. Maybe our experiences are recorded energetically with the organ or gland or even system closest to their vibration. So we have venting our spleen, of all the gall!, spewing bile, bad blood, hot blood, ice water in the veins, hard heart, soft heart, good heart, warm hearted, and so on.

It is possible that I have registered and stored some negative emotions in my body. Such as being pissed off at somebody. Or even being chronically pissed off, as in, "It is raining today just to interfere with my personal plans, and for no other reason." There is even another theory, a corollary to #53, stating that organs which are overloaded with negative emotional debris can become impaired in their physical function. When our organs are overloaded processing our emotional stuff, especially if we aren't helping any, they can become troublesome. You could imagine this like an old telephone switchboard, all the lines are engaged - plugged in, nothing else can get in or out. I find it interesting that joyous emotions don't need to be "processed".

In the treatment sections we will go into "metaphysical" or emotional physiology - emotional or energetic correlations to physical organs or glands in the body. I find the workings of the body fascinating, especially the complexity and interrelated balance, and these energetic correlations make sense to me. I often use them as a basis for creating affirmations, a starting place for change, especially in attitude or approach to healing. These metaphysical correlations are not meant for diagnosis (we don't diagnose in Reiki, remember) or as literal cause and effect (Reiki addresses the cause whether we actually know what it is or not, be it physical or metaphysical). These suggested correlations are simply information and one more aspect which may be considered in a holistic approach to healing. In general, I find the more reaction I have to a particular suggestion, the more I need to look at it.

Along this line, then there is the garbage can theory (#94, I believe, more about that later on). It states that it takes an enormous amount of energy to keep the lid on a garbage can full of emotions, one that hasn't been cleaned out in say, thirty years or so. You could think of this as an over packed suitcase, if you'd rather. One you have to sit on to get closed, but you still keep adding one more item. Well, here's another wonderful thing about Reiki.

Reiki energy is that light vibration, remember? It is that healing and balancing energy that doesn't require our help or direction to bring balance and healing to the body. Reiki energy is so pure, it dissolves any negatively held energy, often without the memories having to make the trip up to the language centers in the brain to be put into words or images in order to be recognized and released. Reiki facilitates the release right at the vibrational level. Sometimes I envision this like those sonic cleaners that dissolve debris in intricate rings and things. You put the jewelry in the apparatus, turn it on, and the crap drops off, leaving the rings and things in glowing, pristine condition.

OK, I understand about the good vibrations now, you may be thinking. So now what? Well, Reiki is a vibrational energy that brings other vibrations into harmony. Keeping this in mind, we can go on to this idea of being an energy body.

Energy Bodies

In class I ask my students (I always say, "God forbid! Erase! Erase!" before I start) "Would I still be Penelope if I lost a leg? Would I still be me?"

Eventually they answer "Yes." Then I go on, "What if I lost the other one? Would I still be me?" I explain I would be shorter, of course, and that if I had a skirt on, they might not even notice. They eventually allow that I would still be me.

Then I go on, "What about my arm? Would I still be me if I lost my arm?"

I explain that if I were on the telephone with them, they wouldn't even know if I had all my original equipment in terms of body parts. Eventually they allow that I would still be me if I were missing a few parts.

So I go on to ask, "How far could this go, and I would still be me?" Like an old science fiction show, I could end up a brain in a bottle, a disembodied voice. What's the point?

Well, the point is, I am not my body. I dearly love my body, and I am eternally grateful for having it to live through, healthy, happy and intact. I can certainly do more things with it than I could do without it, especially on this plane. It is certainly a part of who I am. And -

I am more than my body. Actually, my body changes with every breath I take. Thousands of cells die, and thousands more are created. Within a year, most of my cells are new. Within seven years, they have all been replaced, I have an entirely new body, cell-wise. What keeps the cells replacing Penelope? Why don't I evolve into Martha or Claude? And how do I maintain my memory? And how does my immune system maintain the information that I had the measles when I was nine?

There has to be something else at work here - something unchangeable, something constant. If I am not my body, then what exactly am I? I'm probably not my mind, God knows I can change that. I'm certainly not my brain, that is just a functional part of my body, albeit a really important part. It keeps me breathing and my heart beating while my mind is on other things, like writing this sentence.

So, what exactly am I? Here's what I think.

I think I am an energy body that lives in and through a physical body. I think my mind is the thinking part of this energy body that uses the brain functions to keep everything running smoothly, facilitate growth and evolution. I think this energy body is wholly and perfectly present in each and every cell, something like a hologram that is present entirely in each fragment of the negative, even if it is shattered. I think this energy body is the intelligence that, like a blueprint, works through my DNA and RNA in my cells to keep reproducing Penelope. This process will continue until death of the body.

I think this energy body is made out of and innately connected to divine intelligence, and that I can be in conscious touch with this intelligence when I can quiet my mind long enough to hear it. I think this divine intelligence knows a lot more than I do, and in many dimensions, and has the ability to guide me along my highest path if I am willing to receive the guidance and direction.

Another thing about energy bodies: my energy body is perfect. So is yours.

Kirlian photography, a particular form of photography that shows energy fields, illustrates that if you cut a piece off a leaf, the energy field of that leaf remains intact. This is important. If a person has a body part removed for any reason, the energetic whole of this person still exists. Actually, if you are treating an amputee, they can tell you where your hands are on their body - the part that is physically missing. This is especially effective in treating "phantom" pain. And in treating organs that have been removed. Try it. It works.

Kirlian photographic technique was originally used to detect illness in crops - differences would show up in the energy field several days before any physical changes in the actual plants. This is an exciting thought. What if imbalances actually do show up in the energy field first? Maybe we can treat them there, balancing the energy field may actually prevent physical manifestation of an illness. Or - by bringing the energy field back to balance, perhaps the effects of physical manifestations of illnesses can be mitigated, or even healed.

Now, how is it that my energy body is perfect? Well, another thing about Kirlian photography: in photographing leaves of the same species of a plant around the world it was found that the energy fields of healthy plants are exactly the same, and the energetic field itself has a perfect form.

I understand this as something like a holographic image - each of the cells in our body has the same DNA and RNA - sort of like a condensed blueprint for our entire body is present in each one of our cells. Theoretically, an entire person can be cloned from a cell - all the information for building the entire body is present.

So, if we think of each of our cells as a miniature movie projector, each cell is projecting the same three dimensional picture - ourselves in our perfection, according to the original blueprint, before any additions, subtractions or changes were made. This actually creates a living hologram - a three dimensional energetic version of ourselves made according to the original, perfect in concept, blueprint. Our physical body is just a denser version of this energetic one.

Personally, I think this is one of the ways healing occurs in the body. When we are out of alignment with our original blueprint, it is possible to remind the body of what it is in its "perfection"; the dis-ease, or dis-harmony can dis-appear as our physical body comes back into alignment with our "perfect" energy body (like the sonic cleaner, the crap drops off). We just needed to remind our body of its innate perfection, of where the unhealthy "additions" were added to the original, whether it was attitude, habit, substance, injury, whatever.

In case you are thinking this may be another version of "blaming the victim for the manifesting dis-ease", sort of a New-Age attitude game, let me assure you it isn't. It is about responsible and whole-istic approaches to healing. I once gave a Louise Hay book to a woman with cancer. She called me back, somewhat hurt and angry. "I didn't create my own cancer," she said flatly. She felt blamed for her disease after reading this particular book. I explained that I was sorry she had taken the information that way. Louise Hay simply looks at the possible correlations between emotional/energetic attitudes and physical manifestations of dis-ease or dis-harmony. Healing often occurs when emotional attitudes are changed, physical manifestations of illness are often released along with underlying attitudes and even belief systems which seem to support them.

There is a lot of debate about this approach. My personal opinion is that if nothing changes, nothing changes, so my personal belief system supports paying attention to energetic and emotional healing along with the physical. What have you got to lose, besides an attitude or two? And, it might be helpful.

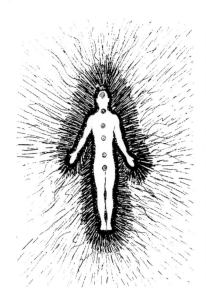

Back to the energy body. I don't think this energy body stops at, or is contained by my skin. It would be like trying to keep water in a paper sack. It will seep through. I think this energy body extends beyond my skin and makes up what some people call an energy field or an aura. I don't think that it is simply heat that is photographed with infra-red cameras. And I know it is energy that shows in Kirlian photographs. And isn't it funny that the energy of the human body, when photographed this way, looks exactly like the chi maps that Chinese physicians have been using for a couple thousand years? Some people call this energy body the spirit or soul.

So, if this energy extends beyond my skin, where does it stop? Actually, I don't think it does. This energy has three major phases, layers or dimensions (we are actually inter-dimensional beings). There are finer divisions and definitions, we'll just discuss the major ones here.

From within my body to a few inches beyond my skin, this energy is thick, almost like Jell-O, if you could imagine energetic Jell-O. Only people we love, or trust, or pay as a professional, like a doctor or a masseuse, touch us in this space. I call this our personal energy space, and it is the first layer of our energy field.

Extending out two to three feet is the next layer, something like thin Jell-O. I call this cocktail party space, because it is how we know if someone is safe to be around. This layer can actually expand and contract, and is part of our natural boundary system, our protection. Your energy field contains everything you are - molecules from your physical/chemical composition and vibrations from your emotional makeup.

When two people meet each other, it is actually their energy fields that "read" each other and tell the person the most about the other, without any words. This is the basis of our "gut" feeling about somebody. Our energy field reads theirs, and vice versa, in its entirety and gives us the kinesthetic report immediately, with the bottom line - this person is safe to be next to or not. Listening to our gut reaction is another matter. Sometimes we have to re-train ourselves to really pay attention.

So, on the energy field level, there really are no secrets and we really can't tell any lies. It is just ego, mind, training or old belief systems that make us think we can. We might just as well begin living our truth because it is there for all to feel or see, anyway.

The third layer of this energy field stretches out to infinity. It is still part of your energy field, connected by vibrational energetic force, like the atoms, remember? Of course the molecules of our field, close together within us, are maybe light-years apart in the outer reaches. Our energy field blends with that of all other living things, and becomes part of that greater energy field we call Universal Life Energy, Divine Presence, or, by any name, God. This is the collective energy that contains everything. This is the energy we call on to filter out and bring through the balancing, healing band or vibration that we call Reiki.

So this explains why some philosophies claim we are each the center of our own universe, we actually radiate out from our center. This explains why we can say a prayer or "send" Reiki to a person and they actually receive it the instant we send it - it doesn't "go" anywhere, you see. We are all in the same energetic soup – prayers, blessings, healing occurs for another person at the same moment we create it in our consciousness - think of it ourselves with the intention of "sending" it along. This may even explain how electricity, television and radio work, but I don't know those explanations, so that won't be covered here. (Am I hearing a sigh of relief?!)

Well, out of philosophy and into more practical miscellaneous items.

One Way Flow

During a Reiki treatment, the Reiki energy flows only one way. Like water through a hose or toothpaste from a tube, Reiki energy comes through the practitioner to the recipient. There isn't any backwash. You cannot take anything on from the person receiving a Reiki treatment. And remember the flow of Reiki energy is catalyzed by the recipient's ability to pull it through, not the practitioner's prowess or ability to "give".

Tracking

So, Reiki energy flows in one direction. That said, there is a phenomena called tracking which can sometimes happen to the Reiki practitioner while giving a Reiki treatment. My body sometimes tracks while I am giving a Reiki treatment. I'll explain tracking to you, so you'll know what it is in case your body tracks also. You can think of this as the tuning fork phenomenon - a still tuning fork will vibrate when brought into the vicinity of a tuning fork that is already vibrating.

Tracking is when my body will let me know how another person is feeling by reproducing that feeling within me. I know the feeling isn't mine, because I didn't feel that way when I sat down to do the treatment. I simply thank my body for being so sympathetic and efficient in its ability to tell me what is going on, and either imagine that the discomfort dissolves as soon as I have recognized what it is (like the telephone stops ringing when you answer it) or I let the discomfort be washed away with Reiki. I picture it leaving my body through my feet, and following my energetic roots into the earth. Some people think of this as "grounding" the energy, like a safety ground (or earth) wire on an electric socket or appliance.

Tracking is *not* "taking on the disease" of another. This is an entirely different phenomena and form of healing, more in the psychic realm, and I do not recommend it. This form of healing stems from the belief that one person has a higher vibration than another, and can take on a disease and transform it and release it from/through their body. Even if this could work, I do not see the wisdom in it - it is an external fix, and does not encourage the recipient's body to heal itself.

This is another thing I love about Reiki - Reiki supports, catalyzes and empowers the recipient's body to do its own healing, strengthening the body to take care of itself in the situation at hand and in general in the future. This is what healing is about for me - empowering the person to heal themselves.

Emotional Energy in the Body

I envision emotional energy being held or used in the body one of two ways:

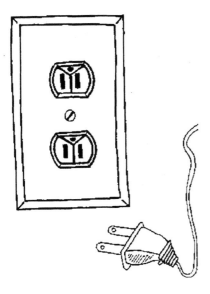

1. Energy is like the electricity in the wall. It doesn't make any moral judgments about how I use it. I just plug some apparatus in and it functions. So the greater energy doesn't care if I use it to bless somebody, or to curse them; to fill myself with feelings of forgiveness or with resentment. That is all up to me. Of course, I do have to deal with the consequences of how I use the energy in/through my body/mind/spirit. If I am in pain because I have used energy for anger, for example, I can simply "unplug", and quit using energy for this purpose. As soon as I unplug, the energy becomes neutral again.

2. Like turning on a light in a darkened room, Reiki dissolves any negatively held emotions. Light dissolves darkness. Darkness cannot exist in the presence of the light. Reiki is a light vibration.

Reiki energy can dissolve and/or release painful memories and/or emotions, without our even being aware of what they are. They don't have to take the trip up to the brain to be converted into audio or video memories for our perusal before we release them. They can take that trip if necessary, of course. However in my personal experience, when I convert the memory in order to review it, I sometimes get caught up in re-living the situation and feelings, and I decide to re-store the whole thing rather than deal with it, for one reason or another. Then I have to go through the process all over again some other time. (A lot like dealing with my junk mail or my storage closets.)

Sometimes it seems I just want to remind myself that I've been hurt, and how bad that felt at the time. I mean, who else will witness my pain if I don't? Somebody has to remember that this or that happened, and how awful it was, somebody has to keep score, don't they? The problem here is, I already decided to be hurt once, when whatever it was happened. So, why re-live it? I probably recorded the lesson for future use, at least I hope I was paying attention and became objective after the pain was past - something useful like, "No matter how angry you are, remove your hand from the door case before slamming the door." I probably already had a difficult time deciding whether or not to release the situation and/or the persons involved. It feels like I've been here before, it smells a lot like old garbage already. Maybe I could consider letting it go.

Garbage Day

Speaking of old garbage, here's the Garbage Can theory (#94, remember?). Friday is garbage day in the town of Schuylerville, New York. If it is Friday, and there are black plastic bags with little pink stickers on them lining the street, I can be fairly sure these bags contain garbage. I could go out and open each and every one, inspect them closely, and determine that they are actually filled with garbage, or I can trust that this is so, let the bags be carried away and get on with my life.

I treat a lot of my negative emotional memories that way. I am not discounting these memories, or the pain that I may have experienced in acquiring them. I simply ask myself what my goal is. If my goal is to prove that life isn't fair, or that I was really right and they were really wrong, or that I really got hurt, then I can go through my negative emotional memories like I go through a photo album - this picture reminds me of this time or incident, that picture reminds me of that time in my life. Eventually it will occur to me that the emotions brought up all end up feeling pretty much the same - painful.

What to do?

I could go through and sort these emotions all out into categories and incidents like recycling the garbage, if I want – cans go here, cardboard goes there; betrayal goes here, resentments go there. If I learn from this exercise, notice patterns that I can change, then this is a productive thing to do. If I don't learn, or get lost in the exercise, I could be in trouble. See, sorted or not, I don't ever have to release them. These incidents and emotions can be kept like articles in a time capsule. They can be trotted out forever to support this or that belief system, prove this or that conclusion about the workings of the world, and, incidentally, call more of the same experience to me so I can continue to prove how right I am.

Of course, I could take another approach. I could assume that even sorted, these negative incidents, emotions and conclusions are not serving me. I could take a leap of faith and let them all go, in a black plastic bag with a pink sticker, this Friday.

My personal goal in this lifetime is to come out even - not owing any karma (needing to discharge "bad" actions with good actions or vice-versa). I want to fully balance everything. If I have offended someone I want to make amends the best way I can as soon as possible, just so I don't have to carry that incident around to feel guilty about until I do something to rectify the situation. And I know my mind is excellent at remembering things I should feel guilty about, so there isn't any cheating.

If someone has offended me, I want to forgive and release them as soon as possible - simply because I don't want to have to carry around either their weight or the weight of what ever they did. I'm going to allow right away that I feel hurt, if I do. I'm going to witness my own pain and then I'll ask myself how long I'd like to carry it around. I'm going to allow that I can change my feelings, if I'd like, right now. I can do this through understanding and forgiveness, or simply turning it all over to a higher power if I don't feel capable of understanding or release. Done.

Forgiveness and Release

I used to work a lot with people in Twelve Step programs, and people who had been abused in one way or another. I used to spend a lot of time assuring them that there really was a place beyond their pain and even their anger, and that the path through their pain was by way of for-give-ness - giving it over, releasing it. There is even a place beyond forgiveness and release. That is a place where no forgiveness is necessary because we recognize that we are serving each other in learning our lessons, and that we are all, in our own ways, serving the Divine. One step at a time.

I read this book by Catherine Ponder once, "The Dynamic Laws of Prosperity", and it changed my life. It was a book on prosperity, but it talked a lot about forgiveness and release. I took a couple of her prayers and personalized them into affirmations for myself. I use them daily:

I forgive and release absolutely everyone and everything in my life that can possibly need forgiveness and release, including myself, in body mind and spirit; in life, work and surroundings; in all time space and dimension. I am free and you are free. I release you in love and fill these spaces with unconditional love.

I bless you and I bless you, _____, for the goodness of God that is at work in and through you as it is in and through me. I claim for you as I claim for myself that the goodness of God is all that exists in this or any situation, and all else is now and forevermore dissolved. I am free and you are free. I release you in love, and fill these spaces with unconditional love.

Of course I use Reiki to fill the spaces with unconditional love, because that is what I think Reiki is. You don't have to mean these affirmations to use them. I tell students that they can grit their teeth while repeating them, even insert "I bless you and I bless you, you jerk," (or whatever they are calling the person at the moment). Just get started. The only thing you have to be willing to do is make a step in a positive direction.

I like to say these affirmations out loud because I believe there is a power in the spoken word, so I take Buster the dog for a walk in a local cemetery. Nobody cares if you talk to yourself in the cemetery. Or if they do, they tend to leave you alone to get on with it.

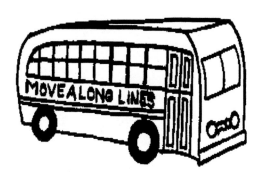

I have another method I call "Bitching About The Bus Trip". I use it for myself as well as some of my counseling clients. I will witness your pain once. I will hear your full story once. This is the bus trip you took to get to this place in your life. Now that you are here, at age whatever, in Schuylerville, New York, on this bright and sunny day, what would you like to do with your life? How would you like to go forward? What, if any, baggage do you wish to take off the bus and carry along with you? Who would you like to travel with on the next segment of your journey?

As Willie Nelson and Kris Kristofferson (two of my favorite poets) say - "what matters is what happens from here to the end."

If you want to keep re-living your bus trip, I will very kindly shake your hand and wish you well, and let you go. If you would like to get off the bus and go forward in your life, I'm happy to walk a ways with you. I'll even give you a garbage bag and a pink sticker when you get tired of your excess baggage.

Know Your Depth

Speaking of counseling, first know your place - counseling is not a part of a Reiki treatment. Then, know your depth. Reiki can allow lots of emotions to surface, and is often used as a support in talk therapies. It facilitates and supports the process in a very clear way. However, unless you are a therapist yourself, you don't get to participate. If I feel a person would benefit from another form of therapy, I recommend them to someone else, as I would recommend them to a physician if I felt they needed to be seen by a medical doctor.

I am gentle in the way I approach these subjects. In the case of a physician I might say, "I wonder when you last had a check-up? I ask because I noticed ____ during the treatment. Have you any thoughts or information about this? Of course it could be anything, and if it were me, it is something I would mention to my physician during a check-up."

If I feel a client is having a difficult time emotionally, with grieving for example, I would give them the name of a specialized therapist, or at the very least tell them that such people exist. I only recommend therapists by name if I have had direct contact with them and like them and how they work, of if they have been recommended to me by more than one close friend or client whose judgment I trust.

In England, the responsibility to refer a client to a physician is actually covered by law. A person may opt to treat a condition with alternative therapies, but the therapists must inform the clients that they can, and perhaps should, see a physician. It is a good practice.

You are not allowed to diagnose, or to prescribe anything to anyone, unless you happen to be a physician. And it is best to be really careful about what you recommend or suggest. Some people are highly suggestible in any event, but may be even more so in the energy of trust and healing that is generated by a Reiki treatment.

I do not normally speak to a client during a Reiki treatment. If a client shares what is going on for them during a treatment, I may answer, "Really?" If it seems a more substantial statement is required, I may answer, "Oh, really?" I find this three word vocabulary, with the occasional addition of "Yes", "No", or "Hummm" covers most situations.

In most cases, "Hummm," will be sufficient. They really just want to know I am there and listening. I understand that it is tempting to give the person the benefit of your opinion and advice, especially since they seem so vulnerable and are such a captive audience, and may even have asked you - but do everyone a favor and resist the urge. Reiki works whether you talk or not, and usually better if you don't.

Remember that the person is actually deeply relaxed, even in an altered state something like meditation, and you have responsibility for what happens while they are under your care. If a client asks directly for my opinion during a treatment, I will usually say, "Let's talk about that later."

By later I mean after they are sitting up, and have put on their shoes and are having a cup of tea. They are much less vulnerable this way. This allows them to receive their Reiki treatment in silence, and allows Reiki a chance to support whatever clarity is emerging within them. Empowering them to heal themselves, remember?

Rule of threes

There are times when you may feel called to bring something to a client's attention. The rule of threes is my way of checking with myself about whether or not I should speak to my client about something I feel in their body. If I feel something strongly three times, it is possible that I'm supposed to bring this to the person's conscious attention in language, so they at least have the option of exploring it further. Here's an example.

Once while giving a treatment to a lady I noticed some unmistakable signs of thyroid imbalance. I was concerned, but didn't want to alarm my client unnecessarily. My "gut" kept telling me something was wrong, and that I needed to speak. I waited until we were done and then I asked the lady when her last physical was. She said, "About thirty years ago, why?" So I went through the, "It may be nothing, and I notice some changes in the texture of your hair and skin, and this sometimes signals an imbalance in the thyroid. It might be good if you break with your long-standing tradition, go get a physical and ask the doctor to include a thyroid test. It couldn't hurt."

She really didn't want to see a doctor, so she contacted a friend who worked in a local hospital and arranged an illicit blood test. The results showed a serious imbalance in her thyroid levels. She called and asked me what to do next. "Do you speak another language besides English?" I asked. "No," she replied. "Then I strongly suggest that you make an appointment with a physician and ask, in English, to have your thyroid levels checked."

It turned out that the doctor was reluctant to order the tests, and she finally had to tell him about the illicit one. He ordered another test, and the thyroid levels were seriously off. She was given medication and was back to normal in a couple of months.

On the other side of the coin, another time I gave a treatment to a woman who had had a bout with cancer the previous year. As I was treating her hips, I felt what I understand to be a huge amount of pain, it really caught my attention. I had felt that kind of pain recently in another client who had cancer in the bones, which had metastasized from another site in the body.

After we were finished with the treatment, I asked this woman about any follow up treatments for the cancer. She said that she had opted for surgery alone, no other treatment, and that she had discontinued seeing her doctor because she had no medical insurance. I said I was concerned about what I perceived as extreme pain around her hips, and urged her to consider seeing her doctor again for a checkup.

She then told me she used to be a dancer, and that the pain I felt was arthritis, it had been there for a long time, and was one of the reasons she quit dancing. I was relieved, but she was quite upset. It was one of her fears that the cancer might come back, and my comments opened up this dark door again. I felt badly that my clumsy expression of my concern caused her emotional distress.

It can be a delicate balance between speaking your feelings and alarming someone unnecessarily. Check with yourself first - the "gut" test. Try silence, and see if it comes back.

Use the rule of threes. Then if you still feel you need to speak, share any information from a calm and caring space, preferably after the treatment is over. You do have some responsibility for the consequences of what you share and how.

I'm still glad I spoke to the dancer about the pain, but now I would know how to handle this better. I would first ask her for feedback (Is there anything going on with your hips?) and her opinion, and - this is the real important part: I would avoid drawing (or jumping to) any conclusions or venturing any interpretations of cause and effect. That is not my job. Offering Reiki is my job. And that is best done in silence, without my opinions, fears or agendas.

Metastasized cancer seemed a logical inference here, and a real concern, and was really on my mind because of my experience with my other client. And there was another logical cause of this person's pain of which I was simply not aware.

I keep a box of Kleenex handy to wipe egg off my face. And it is true that we humans often learn by making mistakes. We do the best we can. It's OK.

Reiki Practice

Giving Reiki Treatments

Just Reiki

Just do Reiki. If you happen to be trained in other modalities, or another form of therapy, alternative or not, that is fine. Please keep it totally separate from Reiki time and treatments, preferably on another day entirely. I'm sure your other forms are wonderful and effective. That is not the point. If I come to you and you promise to give me a Reiki treatment, that is probably what I expect and what I want. Now you have me on the table, and I am in a vulnerable position.

Because it is in your personal belief system, you call in a few entities or deities with whom I am not acquainted, familiar or maybe even compatible. This may be conducive to your comfort, but not to mine. Let us think about that. Let us consider treatment boundaries, individual feelings, safety, invasion of privacy and sacred trust. How you prepare yourself for a treatment within yourself or before I arrive is your own business - it becomes my business if you are including me in your rituals whatever they may be.

Or - because you are trained in massage, you feel a knot of tension in my neck muscles and decide that it is OK to manipulate it out, after all, it will only hurt for a minute. I thought Reiki was a light hands-on treatment - where is my trust factor now? It was for my own good, you say? You were only trying to help me? Oh.

Or - because you are trained in dream psychology you start to analyze my latest one during the treatment. Or because you are a past life therapist we go there. Or because you are a talk therapist you start engaging my inner child and my Mother issues and I can't drift off to sleep or figure things out for myself. You get the idea.

This is not what I asked for, paid for, or what I expected. And you are not providing what you promised. I know, I know, you may think that if you are providing *more* than what you promised, that is justification enough. Well, not really. If you were providing more of what we contracted for, perhaps. But if you are providing something *different from* what we contracted for, that is really not OK. And it is really not OK to get me on the table and then change your mind about treatment form, and either to go ahead without my knowledge/consent/ permission, or to ask me for these when I am already in a vulnerable position.

Reiki is sufficient, Reiki is enough. I promise you. Quit trying to trying improve it, or prove how good it is, or even how good you are. Release your need to fix things.

Preparing Yourself - Or Not

You don't need to prepare yourself, or do anything special to give Reiki - Reiki knows what it is doing and has a built in intention/design of balance for the body's highest good. And although it is not necessary, some practitioners like to use a conscious statement of attitude and intention to prepare themselves to give a Reiki session. They like to have words, thoughts or a visualization to set the stage for a treatment, to remind themselves that this is a healing time and space. This practice brings attention to the treatment and the person receiving, and it is a lovely thing to do if you care to. You can create your own rituals, thoughts, statements, or here are some thoughts that I like to use:

I open myself to the powers of the light and call upon the highest powers of the Universe to channel healing to me and through me to all that I touch this day, to this person ___ under my hands.

In preparation for a Reiki treatment, I like to remind myself of my innate connection to the energy which surrounds me. I imagine that I am like a tree that walks. I imagine my energy roots extend into the earth, no matter how far that may be. Energy is moveable. I imagine that when I inhale I can actually absorb and breathe up the strength of the earth through my energetic roots. I imagine that my energy field also extends into the sky, and that I can feel the power of the Universe flow through me when I exhale, all the way through my body and feet and into the earth below me.

I imagine that with every breath I take, I receive all the power and strength I can ever use, just by breathing. This connection is innate and has nothing to do with who I am or how I use it. I imagine that the Reiki energy that is coming through me dissolves anything I wish to release, and that the natural energy flow is to release it into the earth where it can be energetically recycled. Remember because of the initiations, only pure Reiki energy comes through my hands to the person receiving.

I envision that the Reiki energy being received by the person under my hands is doing the same for them - dissolving anything they need to release, and the natural flow is allowing it to return to the earth for recycling. This energetic release usually happens without their conscious knowledge - even traumatic memories can be released without going through the brain to be translated into images and words.

Sometimes a person will feel a wave of sadness or even giddiness, and not know what it is about. This signals to me that a very natural, gentle energetic release is going on. I keep my hands on their body to keep the Reiki flowing and facilitate the release, unless they ask me to move on.

I begin the actual treatment by saying out loud to the person, "This time is just for you..." then I usually maintain silence, and in my mind I may run this empowering affirmation:

I bless the Divine within you. This energy is being given to you in Love. If you accept it you may use it for your highest joyful good.

Preparing the Physical Space

You can give Reiki just about anywhere you can bring your hands, they are all you really need. The Reiki will always take care of itself. You can do a few things to assure a comfortable treatment for others, and for yourself as the practitioner.

Here is my list of do's and don'ts for getting ready to give a treatment:

Find a Comfortable Place to Work

First, the setting for a full, formal treatment is important. When I first began giving Reiki treatments to family and friends, I used my kitchen table with comforters for padding. It was the sturdiest place in the house, if not the quietest. After I got a massage table I would either do house calls or work in the living room. Finally I set up a room just for treatment. This is absolutely the best, because the energy feeling remains the same in the room, and the room becomes almost a sanctuary. People feel this when they walk in, and feel safe right away.

I avoid working where I sleep, especially when I am traveling. If I have to, I clear the energy after the person leaves. I use a sheet to cover the massage table or bedclothes, and I always wash it or at the very least air it out between treatments, the same for pillowcases. I don't mind working where other people sleep, and often leave a client resting and slip out unnoticed after the treatment.

For house calls a portable massage table is a plus. If not available, you can use their living room couch. Seat yourself on a footstool, that will usually bring you to the right height, and allow you to move around as needed. A step stool is also handy for people getting on and off a table. You can buy a plastic step stool in a hardware store and carry it in your car. When you are ready to do the back positions, the person can just roll on to their side and face the back of the couch. If they have a bed with no foot-board, they can lie on the bed with their head at the foot of the bed, and you can use a kitchen chair to do the treatment, almost as if the bed were a massage table.

If they are in a wheelchair, they can remain seated. You can do the head positions while standing behind the chair. Then bring a chair to sit beside them to do the chest and back at the same time - one hand in front and the other in back, or stand to do the back positions as far down as you can get your hands. Hospital beds require a high stool to get close enough, I have also used a garbage can turned upside down with a pillow on it (take the garbage out first). Again, the person will probably not be able to turn over for the back positions. You can do those by placing one hand under the body as you do the chest positions with your other hand - like a sandwich.

A dining room or banquet table is usually strong enough to support a person, check it out first, otherwise it could be embarrassing as well as dangerous. You can use blankets for a cushion, or even purchase the foam "egg crate" mattresses which are fairly light, inexpensive and very comfortable. In the United Kingdom, practitioners often use heavy duty wallpaper pasting tables with pads on them - these are made out of wood, are light and easily portable (they fold in half), and reasonably priced. The floor, with or without cushions, is an absolute last resort, at least for me.

Lightning will probably not strike you if you can not cover every position for the allotted time, these are the twelve positions not the Ten Commandments, and sometimes you have to accommodate for circumstances. It is always better if you can follow the form, which covers organs, glands, systems and energy centers directly. And Reiki eventually gets where it is needed anyway, even if you cannot directly apply where you would like. Remember five minutes of Reiki is better than no minutes of Reiki, and that Reiki is cumulative, so do what you can where and when you can, it all adds up.

Make the Setting as Comfortable as Possible

Privacy is a plus. Find a place where you won't be disturbed. Shut off the radio, TV and unplug the telephone. Soothing music is fine if you both like it. Be sure to adjust the volume before you start. I prefer silence, but have given treatments with the TV on to entertain cranky or distractible recipients, and it has been fine. Adjust the lighting if possible, not too bright or dim. Some people can't breathe if you burn incense, so check, or "cleanse" early enough in the day to allow the smoke to clear. A candle is fine if it is safe and not distracting. Try to adjust the temperature if possible, open a window or turn on a fan if it is hot, turn up the heat or get extra blankets if it is cold, for yourself as well as the recipient. Deal with the dog and the cat, and any non-Reiki participants that may be in the vicinity.

Make the Recipient as Comfortable as Possible

Cover the person with a light blanket. Their body temperature will drop within a few minutes of starting the treatment, so even if they are comfortable before you begin, they may become cool shortly after. If I am in my home, I explain where the bathroom is and ask if they need to use it before we begin. I mention what sounds they might hear - that I have children and a dog and a cat. I ask if they are allergic to any of these, otherwise, the dog and cat may wander in and out, but the children will stay out unless there is an emergency. If the recipient is new to Reiki, I briefly tell them what a treatment is like, and about how long it will take. As I begin the treatment, I assure them that this time is just for them, that if the phone rings it is probably not for them and will be taken care of by the answer machine. I explain that I will be silent unless they ask me a direct question that requires an answer. I don't mind conversing during a treatment, but I like to give the person a chance to relax and receive something just for themselves uninterrupted.

Make Yourself as Comfortable as Possible

Try to make sure that none of your body parts will cramp up or fall asleep during the treatment. Adjust the height of your chair or stool, using pillows or cushions where necessary. It is worth the time you take to do these preparations. I like to use a pillow under my arms, so I can lean on it and not the person. I keep a shawl nearby to put on, often my body temperature drops, too, but I can just as easily become too warm with the energy. I always end up taking my shoes off, so now I do that at the beginning. Any movements you make after you start the treatment are magnified and can be really distracting to the recipient, so double check you comfort level before you begin. If you do, however, become uncomfortable while giving a Reiki treatment, you can't hide being uncomfortable, and the recipient will pick it right up. You might as well take the time to adjust yourself before you start.

If you intend to do a lot of house calls, make very sure you have and bring what you need. I make a list of things that I carry in my car - portable table, sheets and blankets, extra pillow and cushions for under arms and knees, Kleenex, step stool and higher stool, and a folding chair just in case there are no kitchen chairs available. If you are wanting to have a professional practice it is good to also carry brochures and/or business cards, and copies of the flyer for the next Reiki event, open house, class.

HANDS - ON

"Hands-on, Reiki on; hands off, Reiki off," was Takata's explanation for how Reiki works at the first level. The hands-on is the most important thing. And hands on yourself are the most important place. That simple gesture is a first step in your willingness to take care of yourself, to take responsibility for yourself and your own healing. So we begin with self healing, and move on to treatment for others.

Treatment of Self

One of the foundations of Reiki is self treatment. The Usui System of Natural Healing is meant to be used by yourself, on yourself, first. Isn't that refreshing? We don't have to do the self-worthiness dance before applying this marvelous energy to ourselves. It is designed to be used for ourselves first, and the best part is that if we do choose to treat another, we receive a treatment while we are giving one.

I like to think of the Reiki energy entering through my crown chakra, coming down the spinal column to the heart/solar plexus chakra, taking a left and a right and coming out my hands to focus the flow. Reiki doesn't simply stop at those chakras. It is a flow of energy. It continues down and through my own body, filling it, and eventually exiting through the feet, taking with it anything we need to release. Before it leaves, it brings balance and harmony to my body/mind/spirit just as it does to the person I am treating.

I teach very much to self healing. It is a basic element of the system. Self treatment is like brushing your teeth. You don't save it up and brush your teeth once a month for an hour. This is not a productive thing to do. Brushing a few minutes each day will clean the teeth and strengthen the gums, and we can possibly keep our own teeth for a lifetime. Doing your self treatment is like that. Waking up a few minutes early each day, we can start our day by balancing our energy, bringing healing to those areas that need it.

It is very easy, and soon becomes a habit, to give ourselves a full treatment every day. If there isn't time for a full treatment in the morning, treat what you can (I do my eyes at least, and any "embarrassing" parts, as I say in class). I can always keep at least one hand on myself while doing simple tasks, like talking on the telephone, or watching TV, or reading.

Doing a few positions before I go to sleep is a great way to end the day, releasing any worries, and allows me to drift off in a peaceful and relaxed state. Added up this is often the equivalent of a full treatment. Remember Reiki is cumulative. You don't have to do a full treatment every time. Five minutes of Reiki is better than no minutes of Reiki, and five minutes at a time adds up.

Reiki is a way to maintain ourselves, bringing ourselves to a balanced state before we take on our daily tasks. Some people in service professions (even if they are fulfilled by their work) tend to give until they are running on empty, and then have to stop to refill themselves somehow before they can give any more.

I picture my Reiki connection like a water hose, rather than a pitcher. If I were serving water from a pitcher I would have to refill the pitcher constantly in order to keep going. When connected and turned on, the hose always has water (energy) within. Reiki pours out of my hands in a focused way, like water coming through a hose - Reiki fills me with energy before the energy flows out in a focused way.

Treatment of Others

Your first degree class is built around the form of treatment: self treatment first, then a full treatment for another person. It is the most you need to know about Reiki at the first level - where to place your hands for a treatment session. By the end of the class you will have heard the explanations, seen the demonstrations, practiced all the regular and auxiliary positions, and experienced both giving and receiving a full Reiki treatment. You will receive a certificate at the end of the class that states that you have learned these things, and are now a Reiki practitioner at the first level. All you need is practice.

General Information

Your touch is exactly that of laying on of hands - no extra pressure is required, desirable, or necessary. "If they struggle, let them up," I now say in my classes, after I once found a student pressing down hard on a recipient. I asked her why she was doing that, and she said she wanted to make sure the Reiki would work. It will work fine, just for today, release all worry.

Hovering -trying to hold the hands up off the body creates unnecessary tension, and feels funny to both the recipient and the practitioner. Simply lay your hands on the body and relax. No stiff fingers. Think of your hands like warm wax - conforming to the shape below them. In general, use your hands like a unit, like a mitten with no thumb. Keep your fingers together, and your thumb beside them, unless the position itself requires a different configuration.

Reiki is done over a clothed body, usually with a thin blanket as a cover. Reiki will go through up to five inches of anything - blankets, a cast on a broken limb, a heavy sweater, what have you. Once you are in contact with the thicker part of the energy field, Reiki does the rest, so you don't need to worry about the thickness of clothing or covers.

In general you will leave your hands in each position about five to seven minutes. Three minutes is the minimum, and ten is about the maximum. Time varies with each practitioner, recipient and circumstance, so you have to feel what is right with each body. To learn your particular time cycle, you can get a willing recipient, and use a clock to time the positions. Stay for the maximum time in each position, but watch the clock and notice when you feel like you would move your hands naturally. You will probably have a steady natural rhythm, somewhere between three to ten minutes, unless there is a particular need in a certain position on the recipient's body.

Most practitioners dispense with the clock after the first few treatments. You may begin to notice feelings in your hands that are indicators of readiness to move on, or you will begin to simply trust the feeling that a particular position is done.

Remember that five minutes of Reiki is better than no minutes of Reiki, and that you don't have to give a full treatment every time you place your hands on a body.

Keep some Kleenex as a cover for the eyes, and to blow a nose if needed. If you have to blow your nose, please go wash your hands before you start again. Please remember to wash your hands before you start, anyway, and brush your teeth if you had onions or garlic for lunch. Please don't directly breathe on people. They don't like it. Trust me on this one. Sit straight, and keep your face out of theirs.

Have water or a thermos of hot tea ready for both of you at the end, and allow a little time for them to "come back to themselves", and put on their shoes before they (or you) leave. You have both been in an altered state, very much like deep meditation. Take it easy. When driving home, everyone else gets the right of way.

Feeling Things, Or Not, In Your Hands

You may or may not feel sensations in your hands as you give Reiki. The recipient may or may not feel anything. If you do feel sensations, they may or may not agree with what the recipient is feeling. Often they are opposite. Just for today, don't worry - you aren't doing anything wrong, and yes, the Reiki is working (assuming you have been properly initiated into the first level of Reiki, in case you are reading this before you attend class).

Theory #42 states that in our society we are not taught to recognize, pay attention to or understand a lot of the physical sensations we naturally feel in our body. Sometimes it is quite the opposite. We are told that we don't feel what we feel - "Oh, that doesn't hurt!" Of course it hurts. Then we get confused - "If that isn't pain, I wonder what is?" After whatever number of years we have spent being confused about, discounting or ignoring all the wonderful messages we get from our bodies, it may take a while to recognize that we actually do feel sensations in our hands and that they actually do tell us something.

I remember feeling tingling in my hands when I first started giving treatments. I spent a long time checking my arms to make sure my hands weren't asleep because I was leaning on a nerve in my arm, or something like that.

I remember giving my self treatment every day, and wondering if my hands were "broken" because I couldn't feel as much on myself as I felt when giving treatment to others. A lot of practitioners say that they feel very little in their hands when giving Reiki to themselves, although they feel the "after image" on their face, or whatever body part they are treating; or they feel the relaxing general effects of Reiki, so they at least know it is working. My English friend Peter Coates tells the story of feeling nothing perceptible in his hands with self treatment until he volunteered to demonstrate Reiki for eight days straight at the London health fair. After that his hands had discernible sensations.

So, again, I think it is practice. Simply doing Reiki allows you to get better at it. Some people feel hot or cold, tingling or aching. Through practice you will find the meanings for your own hand language. Here's what these feelings mean to me:

Hot or tingly can be a sign of a lot of energy flowing. Just hot can be an inflammation of something. This could be an infection, a burn or abrasion, or a chronic aggravation. Cold or achy can be an area of the body that is so stressed that it is going to take time to allow the energy in (something like watering a very dry plant, you have to let some water soak in before the soil will really drink the water in). Keep your hands in place and you will notice the change as the energy flows.

Just cold can mean a cessation of activity. For example, the pancreas of a person on injected insulin, the adrenals of a person on cortisone therapy, or the uterus of a post-menopausal woman. The feeling of a cool breeze on the back of the hand can mean some physical change is going on in the body. Some people feel this signals the presence of the feminine essence of the divine.

If your hands or arms get achy, this can mean that the body needs a quart of energy and can only take in a pint at the moment. I think of it as energy back-up, waiting to be received. You can either leave your hands in position and wait, the feeling will eventually pass as the body takes in energy, or you can lift the heel of your hand up while keeping the fingers in contact, and this slight movement will change the feeling. If your hands are sweaty, regardless of the time you have been in the position, you have finished the position. Move on to the next one.

Remember that whatever you do or don't feel, or whatever the recipient feels or doesn't feel, has nothing to do with the quality of Reiki that is being given and received, or how the Reiki is actually being used.

And whatever you think may or may not be happening is really none of your business. Your "knowing", and a dollar, will get you a cup of coffee at McDonald's. You do not need to regale the recipient with your psychic prowess, or give a continuous commentary on your experience and what you imagine might be happening for them. It is something like talking during a movie. Bad manners. Reiki is an experience, shut up and enjoy it and allow the recipient to do the same. You can intellectualize it later if you must, or simply compare notes on your experience if you both would like.

I generally use a three word Reiki vocabulary. "Um", or "Humm" is my usual response. If it seems that something more substantial is required, I usually say, "Really?" If that is not sufficient, try "Oh, really?" They just want to know I am still there, listening, and paying attention. If really pressed, "That's interesting" usually suffices.

If a person is experiencing discomfort in the treatment, (different from adjusting the physical comfort of pillows, blankets, etc.) I may ask them if they can "be with that" of if they would like me to move my hands, and if they want me to move my hands, I move my hands. If they want to talk I let them, without any interruption. If they cry I do not disturb them to offer a Kleenex or ask them what is wrong. I assume they have not lost the power of speech and will they tell me if they need anything, tissue or comment.

Body Attitudes and Appropriate Touch

Breasts, chests, boobs, tits, nipples and other unmentionable things:

Appropriate touch comes in here. Nobody gets too excited about the head positions, but when we begin to move down the body all sorts of things come up. With an appropriate professional attitude and touch I should be able to lay hands anywhere on the body without raising any concerns of my own or the client's. If there are concerns, I need to examine why. Checking out all comfort levels before beginning any treatment is important.

This is as good a time as any to clean out your general attitudinal closets concerning bodies and healing. Any questions you have about body parts and areas need to be dealt with before you begin hands-on, especially your own attitudes. How do you feel about bodies in general, bodies you treat, your own body? The first place we tend to run into touchy issues is the curve of the female breast.

I personally believe that the breasts are part of the body, and treat them as such. I realize this makes me somewhat of a revolutionary teacher in the hands-on field. I don't think breast cancer statistics in Western cultures are only a result of our dietary differences with the East. I think our cultural attitudes have a direct affect on the diseases we develop. There is even a book out now that links breast cancer with bra-wearing. I never thought of that, but it is possible factor. At any rate, there has been enough cancer, breast and other, in my female relatives to precipitate my taking a good look at emotional attitudes and physical effects.

In America, we use breasts - especially young, firm, fairly large and smooth skinned ones - to sell things like beer, Coca-Cola and cars, among others. I've even noticed a correlation: the baser the product or instinct a product appeals to, the bigger the breasts and cleavage - beer advertisements use bigger breasts than Coca-Cola ones.

This compartmentalization of an area of the body, making it at once desirable and naughty, come here but don't dare touch, unobtainable and titillating is somehow an unnatural thing. And repeated over generations, it can become an unhealthy fixation. I use the word unhealthy on purpose, and this isn't just about our moral health. Our attitudes have physical effects on the body.

If I were a woman, I would begin to wonder what is so wrong about my breasts. Why is so much attention given to them from the first moment they become discernible from my chest muscles?

42

When I was growing up Catholic, we were very carefully taught not to pay any attention to this area of our body, or any other area that had more nerve endings than elbows. If this area of our body got large enough to remain in motion after the rest of the body quit moving, we were to harness the offending parts immediately.

Training bras hadn't quite made the scene yet, whatever the training was about. The 1950's version of that was the circular stitched cotton bras that we ironed to a point in the front, roughly corresponding to the area of the nipple. It didn't matter what shape you were naturally, we all looked about the same after 8 AM, with varying amounts of discomfort.

The next biggest thing I remember about breasts is having my first baby. I was a Navy wife, and delivering in a military hospital. The doctors were all very young, only a couple of years beyond my nineteen. The doctor I had was about six weeks out of medical school. After the delivery he came in with a very large needle. He announced that he would be giving me a shot to dry up my milk. I said I wanted to nurse my baby, and didn't want the shot. He said, "Why, Honey, you'll ruin your breasts!" I said, "Well, what did you think they were for?" He left, totally disgusted, and I got to nurse my baby. That *is* what I thought breasts were for.

I have always included breasts in the self-healing positions. I believe they deal with self nurture, and are part of the heart chakra energy, the milk of human kindness, and all that. I have noticed that other people are not so matter of fact about this area even for themselves, and especially not in treatment for others.

One woman I know had breast cancer and took Reiki training after her mastectomy. I was talking to her several months later and asked her if she was doing her self healing, especially her breasts. She told me she was too embarrassed to touch herself there. I can't begin to say how sad that perception of a body makes me feel. I felt very bad for her and the social, cultural or religious attitude training she must have been dealing with all her life, and was perpetuating for herself.

I don't think it is exactly my job to change people's attitudes about their body, not that I actually could. But it is part of my job to point out that there are other attitudes and perceptions they could hold.

It is part of my job to point out that healing begins at home, with our own body, mind and spirit. It is part of my responsibility to myself to love all the parts of my body, and take care of them as a whole, because that is what they are. It is like watching ripples on the surface of a pond - where do the ripples end and where does the water begin? It is perceivably different and yet indiscernible.

I also understand that there are laws and rules dealing with potentially intrusive and/or abusive treatment, especially in professional situations, that need to be considered and upheld. And in this insurance/lawsuit era, esoteric concerns often take a back seat to the workings of the "real" world. Male practitioners are more in jeopardy of being accused of sexual impropriety in a treatment on a female than a female practitioner is in a treatment on either sex, although all of the above can happen. Perceptions differ, and can be greatly influenced by a person's own issues and belief system - their social, cultural, religious filters, often some of the same attitudes and beliefs that underlie illness and dis-ease.

This brings up about a thousand questions about attitudes, ethics, professionalism, proper practitioner/client relationship, charging for treatments or accepting "offerings", advertisements, promises of results, etc., etc., etc.

There is also the very real concern that the person we are treating is in somewhat of an altered state during the treatment. If I am working with a new female client (men don't seem too concerned about this area), I will often ask if I may work on her breasts. Once I asked a Reiki Master this and she replied, "Why would you want to?" I answered, "Because they are there." Then we both laughed because they were quite large and very apparently there. When I asked another woman of the same stature, who was being "the perfect chest" for the chest demonstration during a class, she replied, "My pleasure!" and everybody had a good laugh.

These examples simply highlight that there is a lot of "stuff" about breasts and bodies, stuff we are better off releasing. I know it would be easier to ignore all of this, and simply exclude any "iffy" areas. And yet I feel I would be derelict in my duty as a healing teacher to allow these attitudes to continue unchallenged. So I forge ahead on my campaign to treat the body as a whole without any emotional charge. You don't have to follow. This is something you need to discern on your own.

What you are comfortable with, and what your client, especially a new client, is comfortable with, may differ. In that case, I need to remind you that you can place your hands anywhere on the body and the Reiki energy will eventually get to where it needs to go, even if you are not treating that area directly. So you can work within your own and your client's emotional comfort zone and you are giving full treatment - you are not impairing the treatment or its effects in any way. You are actually supporting the treatment by keeping you both emotionally comfortable. This is just as important as physical comfort for both practitioner and recipient.

In general, I treat all bodies the same when they appear on my treatment table. There may be some differences in length or girth, ability to turn over or not, but other than those minor concerns, they are the same. They are a person rather than a male or female. I really don't recognize a sexual difference, because I'm not concerned with their sex unless there is a particular problem that draws my attention to their sex. Then it is still clinical.

I have treated men with testicular cancer, as well as women with breast cancer. I may ask them if they would like me to treat the affected area. I explain that I don't have to place hands over the affected area because the Reiki energy will get there anyway, no matter where I place my hands. I use the same matter-of-fact approach I use if a person has some physical discomfort come up during a treatment. If they are uncomfortable, or prefer that I move my hands, I move my hands. Simple.

I offer to treat the affected area for a lot of reasons. First and foremost the person may be having emotional problems concerning the affected area, from fear of the cancer and the site itself to mourning the loss of that part if they are opting for or have had surgery.

This may be the only unconditional loving touch they get in that area. Any other touch may be clinical and possibly frightening - isolating, deciphering or delineating what is wrong as if it were separate, rather than acknowledging that this is a part of a whole person, a functioning body and psyche.

One woman came into class with her sister. I always ask my students to practice with people they don't know so they can have some sense of how different bodies respond to the energy. As the students were moving into the practice section of the class, this woman called me aside and asked if she could work just with her sister. I asked why. She moved her arm and revealed a very swollen breast. She had had a weeping abscess for quite a while, and was concerned about the tenderness and the odor. This was the second abcess she had had. She decided against Western medical treatment this time, and came to Reiki as an alternative.

I asked if she would be willing to work with a (then) Master candidate, Heather Buglear, who was attending the class as part of her training. She was willing, and these women stayed together for the entire class, ensuring that she got to exchange with someone other than her sister, and that she got the privacy and quality of care and attention she required. During the practice sessions, these two women talked a lot about self acceptance, and accepting and loving the parts of the body that are expressing or manifesting a dis-ease. This was one of the best examples I have ever seen of unconditional love given and - what is often harder - received.

Ethics

In case you haven't gathered by now, there are ethics about fooling around with your recipients or clients, unless you already happen to be in an intimate relationship with each other before you learn Reiki.

The ethics are - don't. Your client is vulnerable. They came to you for healing. They trust you, and their trust is sacred. These thoughts guide all of your interactions with your clients/recipients.

There is an imbalance when you give healing energy to another person. Reiki feels exactly like unconditional love. Which Reiki is. You aren't. You are a person giving Reiki. People can get confused by this. They figure that if you are the channel, you are the love. This isn't necessarily so, no matter how much we would like it to be. You probably aren't capable of maintaining a relationship with unconditional love unless you are a saint, or pretty close.

If you insist on pursuing an intimate relationship with a client, and aren't a professional who can get arrested for this, then at least do both of you a favor, and let enough time pass to allow the relationship to truly change to an equal footing, and to get to know each other as people.

Miss Manners refuses to even entertain the possibility of inappropriate touch in a treatment situation. That is a legal matter and is spelled p-e-r-p-e-t-r-a-t-o-r.

About alcohol or other recreational drugs - if you use those, don't indulge before a treatment. If you have a problem with that, you have a problem, check it out.

An addendum - (reverse ethics, or boundaries if you will) I personally don't treat people who are actively drunk or high unless they are in a life threatening situation. For regular treatment I wait until they are straight or sober. It is a personal choice. If they don't come back, they don't come back. In case your Mother didn't tell you, let me be the first: it is OK to say, "No."

And Reiki treatment time is not the time to try to sell anyone your used car or stock options. Keep business, or any other propositions, for another time.

Good common sense, good manners, some consciousness about your own moral, ethical and value systems, sincere caring and right action in the moment should see you through these or any other issues.

Energy Exchange - A Part of the Form

 In class, we discuss energy exchange. This means, honoring your time by charging money or something similar for it. Many people get on their religious high horse about this, misquoting the Bible and waving their "Spirituality is free and healing ought to be," banners. In case you were preparing to do this, lay down your arms and keep reading. You can always unfurl your banner later.

Besides, I am not actually charging for the Universal energy - that is in infinite supply and can be used by anybody, after all. What I am charging for is my time. That is in limited supply, at best I may have another fifty years, and my stamina ain't what it used to be, indefatigable as I am. I get to choose how I use my personal time and energy, and what I charge for it if I intend to exchange it for money.

Money is a basis in all spiritual systems, it just isn't admitted to in polite society. Something like Victorian England, where women had skirts instead of legs, sex wasn't mentioned although it must have been done because babies were delivered by storks and found under cabbage leaves. I could go on with a lot of history and detail here, about spirituality and money, not about Victoriana, but I'll spare us both the effort.

Money is a conscious part of the form of the Usui System for good reasons. Some stories of Mikao Usui speak of Usui practicing Reiki in a beggar's community. In those stories, a lot of learnings came through this time of practice - understandings about honoring another person's path, understandings about physical and spiritual healing and their interaction, understandings about personal dignity, an individual's investment in their own healing, and earning a living with integrity.

There are several concepts at work here, lets explore them. First of all, you as a practitioner are charging for your time, not Reiki energy. Reiki is intangible and free, your time is tangible and worth something. You only have so much of it. You will figure this out as you get older. What you do with your time becomes increasingly more important.

Most of us spend a portion of our time doing something constructive to earn a living. That is, we do some concentrated form of work, which takes time, trade that for money, and trade the money for food, clothing, shelter, and an occasional movie.

We don't call the electric company and say, "Hey, you guys. I'm a spiritual person and I do good works so you should give me my electricity free." You can try this is you want, but in my understanding this is just not how it works. We don't have to approach it this way.

The Universe supports the electric company, too. It supports the electric company by giving us a job so we can pay for our service, with the electric company and everywhere else. The electric company then uses our money to pay its employees, and the energy/money keeps going around.

So, we are supposed to trade our time/skills/services/work for money, it is a socially and universally acceptable thing to do. We have some choice about what it is that we do with our allotted time that we trade for money. Some of us build bridges. Some of us do Reiki.

Sometimes people ask me how I can charge for doing Reiki. I reply that I like to eat and my landlord prefers that I pay my rent on a regular basis. Since this is what I do for a living, I find it helpful to receive money for my time and services. It is an honest exchange. It allows me to live and buy airline tickets to do Reiki classes and trainings.

In class, I ask everyone to practice saying the phrase, "My usual fee is ___.", until they get used to the sound of it. Then they can add, "However, I do do exchanges or trade. Whaddya got?" It should be something useful, and something you like, and somewhere in the ballpark of what two hours of your time is worth. One of the best exchanges I ever made for a series of treatments was for having all my windows and curtains done. Thank you, thank you, Elaine. And another was having my house beautifully cared for - thank you, thank you, Dyna.

To determine what an hour of skilled time is worth in your area, call a hairdresser, a carpenter, a mechanic and a cleaning service, and average them out. Then adjust it to your comfort. My price has gone up over the years, but is still very close to what a two hour service in a beauty shop would be. I started at $35 a treatment at the Reiki I level, plus extra for house calls. I now charge about $75 for a one time treatment, which is at least two hours of my time. Price depends upon the time I spend, and if this treatment is part of a series (which would be $50 each treatment for four or more in a row).

Next concept: dignity. If I don't accept some form of exchange for my time and effort to deliver this wonderful healing energy, I create an energy imbalance. I am not allowing a person the dignity of an exchange - I am making a beggar out of them, and they might not appreciate it. This is actually a form of an ego trip, albeit a spiritual one, which is not a justification in any event. And this energy imbalance may affect the way a person accepts and uses Reiki.

First, people will value my efforts somewhere near where I value them. If I give them away, they may be received as worthless since they seem to be worthless to me. A friend of mine taught me about this. We used to be married.

We lived on a small farm, and we grew vegetables every year for part of the rent and for freezing and canning for our own use. When I would pick the fresh vegetables, I would often drop off a bag of this or that to friends who mentioned they would like some. My husband objected to this. We certainly had enough to share, and I never understood his attitude.

So, one day he asked me to go for a ride with him. He drove past a friend's house and asked me if I noticed the bag on the porch. It was the same bag of vegetables I had left there several days before. It hadn't been touched, I could tell by the wilted Swiss Chard sticking out of the top. He said, "If you had even charged them a dollar they would have made sure to use them."

Then I understood. I continued to share fresh vegetables, but only when people came to get them. It was a lesson that serves me to this day. I make sure people really want the gifts I have to give, that they will be appreciated and well used.

Second, people open themselves to receive healing, or to begin the healing process, the moment they make an outward effort to find healing. Often, when I make a doctor appointment, I begin to feel better right away. This is because I have made an outward effort to obtain healing, made a step in the direction of helping myself.

My body assumes the doctor will give me something to make it all better, so my body gives itself permission to begin healing and healing starts. It is the act of taking care of myself that begins the work. This act will cost me both time and money, and I am making the effort and investment. I'm invested in getting well. My body understands this, pays attention and responds.

I can still give Reiki as a gift when and where I choose, as long as I am clear in my offering so people can say yes or no. I walk into a hospital room and announce, "You don't need more dead flowers, I'm here to give you a Reiki treatment." I often give demonstration Reiki treatments, especially to journalists who want to write about Reiki. Unless they have experienced a treatment, they cannot write with a full understanding. I tell them the price is right - free - its a limited time offer, take advantage now. I often give medical people the same courtesy.

Of course I treat my family and occasionally trade treatments with friends. For long term treatments, even family members may pay something. It takes time no matter whom I treat, and house call time is a consideration as well in most cases - driving to the home, setting up the table and/or the space, packing everything away and getting back home. House calls often double or triple treatment time. Long term treatments, from five to thirty or more in a row, require a different commitment on my part as well as for the recipient. I have to promise to be there for them so many consecutive days or weeks. They have to promise to be there to receive.

Some people are new to the concept of charging for their time, or feel that they need to practice awhile before they begin to charge for Reiki sessions. This is fine. If it feels more comfortable for you, you could set a number of treatments, say ten full formal treatments, that you will give as practice treatments. I'd suggest that they be with different people if possible, for the experience of how Reiki feels with different bodies.

You could then be very clear in setting up sessions, "You are in luck. I just took this Reiki training and I need to give ten practice treatments to different people before I start charging. I'd be happy to give you one if you would like." At some point you can work in the information about how much your usual fee will be when your practice sessions are complete. Some of these recipients will possibly become clients if you are intending upon becoming a professional Reiki practitioner, so it is a good deal for both of you. And remember charging can be in the form of an agreeable energy exchange.

For a professional Reiki practice, I am now suggesting one hundred formal (preferably paid) treatments as a basis for professional practice. I ask that these be documented – name (unless privacy is an issue), dates, times and settings (such as hospital, house call, treatment center, etc.). I do not keep (or even take, unless the person feels strongly they want me to know) personal information such as presenting problems, because I do not feel this is any of my business, as it might be if I were a masseuse or an herbalist.

TREATMENT

POSITIONS

#1. Eyes

 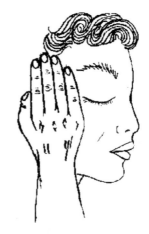

2a. Temples

2b. Jaws

TRADITIONAL HAND POSITIONS FOR SELF TREATMENT

Where to put your hands on yourself for daily treatment, and the physical functions these positions directly affect. For more detailed information, look under the corresponding areas in the Traditional Hand Positions for Treatment of Others.

These positions are only a guide. You basically start at the top and work down, or at the bottom and work up, placing your hands wherever they feel called to be, from three to ten minutes in each position. The object is to get hands on yourself to give yourself a treatment every day. These positions are simply the most logical way to proceed. There is no way to do Reiki wrong. Remember that Reiki gets where it is needs to go eventually no matter where you put your hands, that five minutes of Reiki is better than no minutes of Reiki, that consistency is a key, that the effects of treatment are cumulative and several five minute sessions in a day add up.

1. *Eyes -* palms over the eyes, heel of the hand on the cheekbones, fingers on forehead. (Sinuses, any abnormalities of the eyes, forebrain - perceptions, personality, third eye and pineal gland.)

2a. *Temples -* slide hands to the sides of the face, cheekbones in the palms. ("Oye vey" position, temporal and parietal lobes of the brain, dizziness and nausea)

2b. *Jaws -* slide hands down, jawbone in palms, fingers still in upward position. (Temporomandibular joints - TMJ, teeth grinding)

3. *Occipital and neck -* one hand on the back of the head at the occipital bone and one hand on the back of the neck. (Lying on the beach position; reticular formation, oldest part of the brain, awake-asleep switch, insomnia.)

4. *Throat -* wrists together, fingertips aimed at the back of the neck. (Thyroid, parathyroid, carotid arteries; regulating blood pressure, communication.)

5. *Sternum -* one hand on breastbone, one just above touching the throat. (Thymus and thyroid - immune system, protection, metabolism.)

6. *Lungs -* arms crossed, collarbones in palms, fingertips on shoulders. (Asthma and allergies)

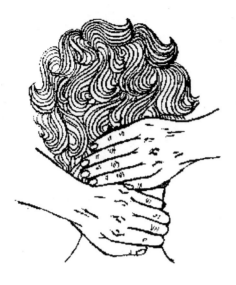

3. Occipital and neck

4. Throat

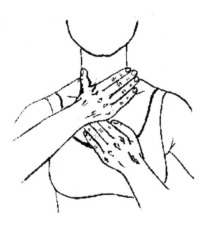

5. Sternum/Thymus

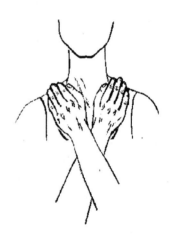

6. Lungs

7. Shoulders (left)

7. Shoulders (right)

54

7. **Shoulders** - left shoulder - insomnia/sleep, right shoulder, gall bladder meridian.

8. **Chest** - above the breasts, fingertips touching over the sternum (accupressure points for release of repressed anger, not that any of us have any of that, of course.)

9. **Breasts** - fingertips touching over heart. (Heart chakra) Auxiliary: arms crossed with fingertips under armpits for chronic lung problems.

10. **Rib cage** - hands under breasts, fingertips touching on solar plexus. Liver, pancreas, spleen, stomach and gall bladder. (De-toxing body, blood diseases, regulating blood sugar)

11. **Waist** - hands across waist, fingertips touching. (Small intestine, transverse colon.)

12. **Hips** - hands below navel and above pubic bone, fingertips meet at "ki" point. (Ascending/descending colon, bladder and either ovaries and uterus, or prostate.)

13. **Kidneys** - hands above waist in back, finger tips on spine. (Filter system of body, cleansing blood)

14. **Sacrum/Coccyx** - hands below the waist in back, finger tips pointing downward on coccyx. (Prostate)

15. **Auxiliary - Inner thighs** - circulation; **knees** - attitudes; **soles of feet and palms of hands** - whole body; **fingertips** - head, sinuses.

There are many places on the body where the entire body is reflected (check out the disciplines of Reflexology, Iridology, acupuncture and accupressure if you are interested). They include the iris of the eyes, the curves of the ears, the teeth, the large intestine, the soles of the feet and the palms of the hands. Often giving Reiki just to these areas is enough to rejuvenate the entire body, for example: hands over the eyes, hands over the lower abdomen for yourself, holding someone else's hand or treating their feet.

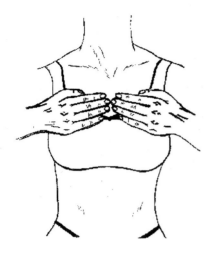

8. Chest -
   Sternum

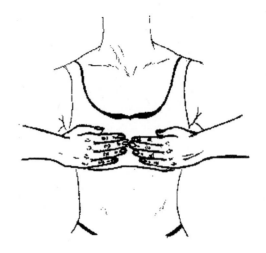

9. Breasts

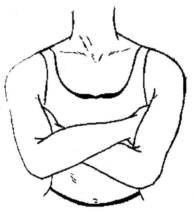

8a. Lower Lungs

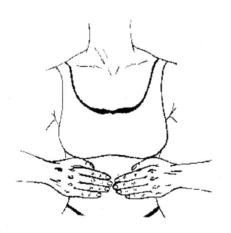

10. Rib Cage

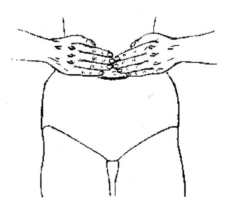

11. Waist

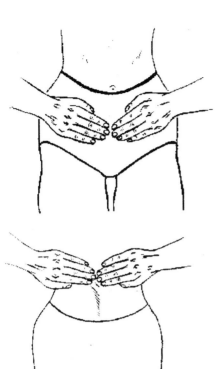

12. Hips

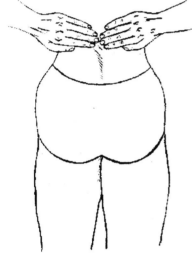

13. Kidneys

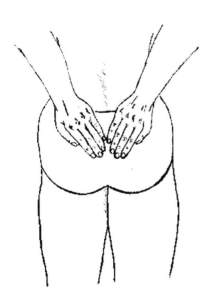

14. Sacrum/Coccyx

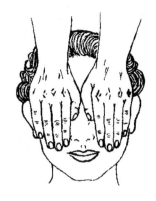

1. Over the Eyes

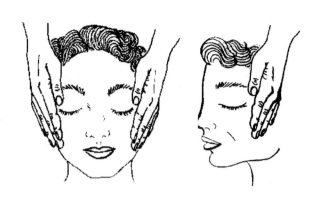

2. Temples

3. Occipital - back of head and neck

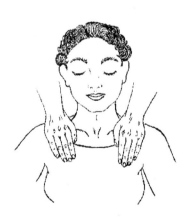

4a. Lungs

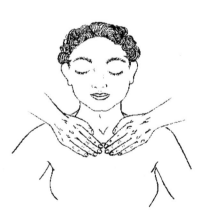

4b. Thymus/Thyroid

4c. Throat

58

TRADITIONAL HAND POSITIONS - SUMMARY
for a basic Reiki treatment given to another person

Sizes of bodies and hands differ, adjust accordingly. For example, don't try to do mini-positions on a baby. There are three sections: head, chest and back; with four basic positions in each section: In general, work from the midline of the body.

HEAD POSITIONS

1. Over the eyes. (Thumbs touch in between eyebrows, fingers along side of nose, forehead is in the palms of the hands.)

2. Sides of the head. (Can be divided into temple and jaw positions 2a. and 2b.)

3. Back of the head. (Sides of hands together, occipital cradled in palms.)

4. Lungs, thymus, throat. (4 a: hands straight, b: tipped in over the thymus, c: temple hands over the throat. Okay, I know this is technically not one position, and not "on" the head, but it all works out in the end, I promise.)

CHEST POSITIONS

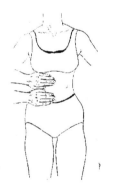 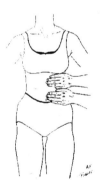  

1. Liver   2. Pancreas/Spleen 3. Small Intestine 4. Ki point

1. Liver. Right side of body.	Hands together.
2. Pancreas and spleen. Left side of body.	Hands together.
3. Across the waist, small intestine.	Hands across.
4. Across the hips, Ki point.	Hands across.

(Hands across - place fingertips at midline, heel of hand on fingertips.

BACK POSITIONS

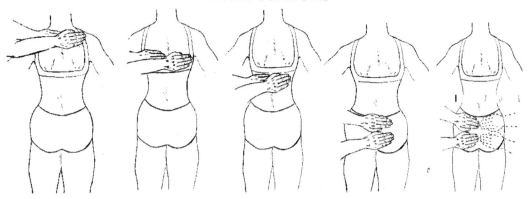

1. Shoulders   2. Adrenals   3. Kidneys   4. Coccyx   4. Coccyx

1. Across the shoulders (high-by the neck).   Hands across.
2. Across the adrenals (under the shoulder blades). Hands across.
3. Across the kidneys (above the waist).   Hands across.
4. Coccyx, (or cheek to cheek, 4a & 4b).   Hands across.

Auxiliary Positions:

1. Under armpits for chronic lung conditions.

2. Any major joint for arthritis.

3. Inner thighs or groin area for poor circulation.

4. Hips - one hand on each.

5. Knees - fronts and backs.

6. Bottoms of feet

HEAD POSITIONS

Head Section, Central Nervous System - A (very) little anatomy and physiology

Before we begin with the head positions, I thought you might like to know what you are working on.

A few weeks after conception, just as the speedily dividing cells begin to differentiate, our brain and spinal cord are formed, which is why fetuses look a lot like commas. The *central nervous system* is formed first, with a sack of fluid around it to support and protect it. This *cerebrospinal-spinal (CSF)* fluid has its own pulse and rhythm, like your breathing or heartbeat. It is the first pulse that we have as the life force begins, and the last pulse to leave us when we die.

There are three membranes or *meninges* that hold this spinal fluid in its own closed system which supports and cushions the brain and spinal cord: the *pia mater* which looks like cling film or Saran wrap, and sticks to the sensitive nerve and brain tissues itself; the *dura mater* that looks like suede and lines the inside of the skull and vertebrae; and the *arachnoid mater* which is full of holes to allow and support the blood vessels and nerves to pass back and forth between the body and the brain and spinal column. The arachnoid mater also acts as a baffle so we don't slosh when we walk. The fluid itself is rich in salts and sugars, so it is a very good conductor of the Reiki energy. Anywhere you place your hands on the head this fluid will be receiving the energy and conducting it to the entire central nervous system - the brain and all the spinal nerves.

The brain itself is basically three structures: the *brain stem*, the *cerebellum,* and the *cerebrum*. The brain stem, containing the medulla oblongata, is an extension of the spinal cord, and is the oldest and most primitive part of the brain. It controls breathing, digestive functions, body temperature, heart rate and blood pressure. The cerebellum is at the base of the skull, controls the skeletal muscles, posture, balance and coordinated movement.

The cerebrum is the largest part of the brain, and is divided into the left and right cerebral hemispheres. The hemispheres are connected by the *corpus callosum*, making it possible to use both sides of the brain at once. Women generally have a larger corpus callosum than men, which may account for "women's intuition" and a more holistic world view, while men are better at single minded tasks. The left hemisphere controls the right side of the body, is linear, deals with logical functions like math and language, and sees in two dimensions. The right hemisphere controls the left side of the body, sees in three dimensions, remembers faces, understands art, music, humor, concepts and stories.

The cerebrum is covered by the *cerebral cortex* which is divided into five lobes: *prefrontal, frontal* (covered by the first head position), *temporal* (position two), *parietal* (position two and three) and *occipital* (position three).

The brain is connected to the head by *twelve cranial nerves* (optic, olfactory and auditory are the sensory, neck and tongue are the motor, the rest are mixed, supplying the head, neck and major organs of the body). The brain is connected to the rest of the body through the spinal cord and thirty one pairs of spinal nerves.

Any of the head positions that touch the skull are good for reaching important structures that lie protected deep within the brain. The thinnest part of the skull is the temple area. The *pineal gland*, sometimes referred to as the third eye, senses Seasonal Affective Disorder, and is best reached from the forehead (first) position.

The *thalamus* (in the center of the brain) is responsible for sorting out the mass of information being fed into the body and passing it on to the cerebral cortex, or other areas as necessary. The *hypothalamus* (in the base of the brain) is the link between the nervous system and the endocrine system, and is concerned with the stability of the internal organs of the body. It controls water balance, regulates appetite, temperature and sleep, plays a part in controlling emotions, and produces releasing hormones that regulate hormone secretion by the pituitary gland.

The *pituitary gland* has two parts, anterior and posterior, and is called the master gland because it produces so many different hormones that regulate or stimulate so many functions in the body it would need its own chapter, I'll spare you the details.

I know this is not technically part of the head, but the fourth head position covers the *lungs, thymus and thyroid*. Lungs are part of the respiratory system bringing oxygen to the cells. The thyroid gland is part of the endocrine system, and produces thyroid hormone which controls metabolism and rates of growth in children.

The *thymus gland* is part of the *lymph system* and deals with natural immunity to diseases. It lies at the top of the thorax, partly over the heart and lungs. In newborns, it controls the development of the spleen and lymph nodes. It produces lymphocytes which are programmed - lock and key - to make antibodies against specific micro-organisms, viruses and bacteria - T cells, T for thymus. Read more about the functioning of the immune and lymphatic systems later on.

Ears have two functions, hearing and balance. The inner ear consists of fluid filled tubes embedded in bone. If the fluid in the semicircular canals keeps moving after the body stops, you get dizzy. For some people, getting dizzy also means getting nauseous, as in motion sickness.

HEAD POSITIONS

Head Position #1: Eyes and forehead

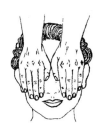

Hands - forehead is in the palms of your hands, tips of thumbs are together between the eyebrows on or above the bridge of the nose, fingertips are alongside but not touching the nose.

Physically: Sinuses, frontal and prefrontal lobes of the brain, pineal gland, any abnormalities of the eyes - cataracts, astigmatisms, glaucoma.

Metaphysically: Frontal and prefrontal lobes of the brain deal with morals, values, decision making processes, belief systems, personality, perceptions. The third eye is actually a vestigial organ and deals with seasonal affective disorder and intuition. Sinuses deal with who or what is "in your face" or up your nose - usually someone or something you are allergic to or that is irritating you on a daily basis - could be chemicals where you live or work, or people you live and work with. I usually find my sinuses have something to do with my own reactions or behavior. (Who, me?) Crown and third eye chakras (energy centers) are located in the head.

Physically: *Sinuses* are basically holes in your head. You have been told you had holes in your head, right? Well, sinus actually means hole. These holes serve to lighten up your skull, which is bone and weighs a lot, and they serve as resonant chambers for your voice. The sinuses are lined with a mucous membrane that is continuous with the entire alimentary canal, all thirty five feet or so. On a good day, these membranes produce a quart of mucous that keeps things running smoothly, so to speak. The sinuses, with the help of the mucous membrane, trap any impurities in the air that you breathe and warm the air before it enters your lungs. Your head feels stuffed up and/or painful if the membranes become irritated or inflamed.

Frontal and prefrontal lobes of the brain are the newest part of the brain, and are what makes us human. These lobes contain mechanisms for the use and control of intelligence and personality, reasoning and abstract thinking, smell, language, speech, and the initiation of movement. They house morals, values, perceptions and decision-making processes. Pineal gland deals with light perception and Seasonal Affective Disorder (depression caused by not enough full spectrum light).

Eyes are the vehicles of our vision. They are made up of the actual eyeball filled with fluid (vitreous humor) that holds a retina at the back, an iris and lens at the front, and a covering (sclera) with a clear part (cornea) that allows light in and keeps the inner workings safe. Any abnormalities in the shape of the eyeball, retina, lens or cornea results in distorted vision. Glaucoma is too much fluid within the eyeball causing pressure on the optic nerve This condition responds well to Reiki.

Head Position #2 - temple and jaw (temporomandibular joint -TMJ).

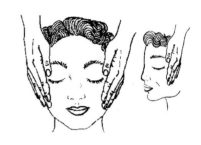

Hands: You can do this position as one by sliding your hands down from the position #1, with the cheekbone in your palms, or you can split this position into 2a and b, depending upon the size of your hands relative to the size of the person's head.

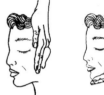

2a. is the upper position, known as "Mr. Spock,." Put two fingers in front of the ear on the temples, and two fingers behind the ear. 2b. is the lower position. The jawbone is in the palms of your hands, the fingertips are on the throat.

Physically: Temporal and parietal lobes of the brain, nausea and dizziness, teeth grinding, temporomandibular joint (TMJ).

Metaphysically: Fears and phobias, courage and cowardice, helplessness and hopelessness, tension, anger, frustration. People with chronic conditions or degenerative diseases can often feel helpless and hopeless without really being aware of it. Sometimes depression can be a chronic condition. Affirmations can be a step in a positive direction. And "false hope" is an oxymoron.

Head Position #3 - Back of the Head, Occipital Area

Hands: Palms cradle the back of the head, little finger alongside little finger, fingertips are on the neck.

Physically: Serves the reticular formation (state of consciousness - awake or asleep), occipital lobes - vision, spinal column. All the scalp and neck muscles insert here.

Metaphysically: Past memories.

This is a very comforting position. Most people fall asleep in this position. They are by now trusting the feeling of Reiki and the consistent rhythm and pressure of my touch. They have adjusted to the sounds and feeling of the room in which we are working, where ever that may be, and are beginning to relax deeply and may even fall asleep.

Head Position #4 a, b, c: Shoulders, lungs, upper chest, thymus, thyroid, throat

Hands:

#4a. Shoulders, lungs, upper chest: fingertips point straight down towards the toes, heels of the hands are high on the shoulders, collarbones are in the palms.

#4b. Thymus: angle hands toward center until index fingers touch over the sternum.

#4c. Throat, thyroid, parathyroid: bring hands up gently, side of thumbs and index fingers rest against jawbone, edge of hand and little fingers rest against collarbones, creating space over the throat.

Physically:

#4a. serves lungs. I know this looks high to be lungs, but I promise they are there. You are also on two major energy meridians of the body, going all the way down to the feet. Meridian is a term used in Chinese medicine to denote an energy channel.

#4b. Thymus is a major part of the immune system, storing white cells from the bone marrow and producing lymphocytes which are programmed to make antibodies against specific micro-organisms - those killer T-cells - individualized lock and key mechanisms to combat viruses and bacteria. The thymus is very large in infancy, controlling the development of the spleen and lymph nodes. It shrinks after puberty, but you can keep it happily active with lots of Reiki, and/or tapping it gently with fingertips - the "thymus thump".

#4c. Throat, Thyroid and Parathyroid Clears Eustachian tubes, do this position first in case of ear infections or blockages especially in children. Balances and stabilizes blood pressure, balances metabolism (thyroid) including cholesterol and calcium levels in blood (parathyroid).

Head Position #4 a, b, c continued: Metaphysically:

#4a. Lungs - intake and acceptance of information. Common site of restrictive emotional "energy bands", especially in asthmatic conditions. You can slide your fingertips under the bands and stretch them. They never return to their original tightness. After several treatments, they may be like the elastic waistbands on Jockey shorts that go through the wash 107 times. When the person stands up, they simply fall off.

#4b. Thymus - this is your emotional immune system and protection center as well as your physical one. You can notice people automatically putting their hand on this area of their chest when they hear something shocking or distressing. It is thought in some disciplines that this is the site of the soul. It is also thought by some that this is the place where your unique vibration is transmitted to the universe, if you were a radio station this is the transmitting tower: station W-Y-O-U.

#4c: Throat - throat chakra is the internal and external communication center. Thoughts pass through here to be manifested as feelings, and feelings pass through here to be interpreted as thoughts. If this internal communication is clear, you at least have a shot at having clear external communication. This is an area we tend to learn to control or even close down early in life, to be able to keep detached from thoughts and feelings. Sore throats can be unspoken words.

I occasionally add an auxiliary position under the armpits for any chronic lung conditions. These usually happen in the lower lungs. Our general tendency is to breathe shallowly rather than deeply. So the bottoms of the lungs do not get exercised or cleaned out unless we do regular aerobic or deep breathing exercises of some kind. Chronic conditions such as emphysema may require chronic Reiki treatments - the condition did not manifest overnight, and will not normally recede in a treatment or two, although I always allow space for miracles to happen.

CHEST POSITIONS

Draw an imaginary line down the middle of the chest, and one across the waist. These are the quadrants in which we will be working. Body and hand sizes differ, so you have to adjust your hand positions to accommodate differences. If you work from the center line you are sure of being over the organs and glands. If a person is a diabetic you may start at position #4 and work up to help circulation. And it is okay to treat them from #1. Hawayo Takata often suggested spending a lot of treatment time here as this area is the "engine" for the body.

Chest Position #1 - Liver and Heart

Hands: Hands side by side in the upper right quadrant, thumbs touching each other, both hands on the liver which lies protected under the rib cage below the breast. Or, one hand above the breast more toward the upper chest, and one hand over the liver. Which position you use depends upon the size/shape of the person you are working on, the size of your hands, and other circumstances, i.e. a colostomy bag.

Breasts: Turn back to *Body Attitudes/ Appropriate Touch* (page 42) to get a full description of the whys and wherefores of treating the breast directly. Basically I like to act as if the breasts are an integral part of the body and treat them as such. However the emotional discomfort level of either the practitioner or recipient may outweigh any possible benefits of direct treatment. Reiki will get where it needs to go eventually no matter where you place your hands.

Physically: Serves heart, gall bladder and liver. Liver is the great inspector and cleanser of the body. The liver detoxes any poisons in the blood; stores iron and fat soluble vitamins A and D, produces bile which assists in the digestion of fats, manufactures plasma proteins including fibrinogen for clotting action of blood, and maintains blood sugar levels in conjunction with the pancreas.

Metaphysically: Heart chakra is about unconditional love. Solar plexus chakra is about unconditional healing. Breasts are about nurturing, especially self nurture. Liver deals with memories of people and unexpressed emotion. We can express emotion in hundreds of ways - through our work, art, cooking, writing, sharing verbally, or whatever. If an emotion, positive or negative, remains unexpressed, it is probably vibrationally stored in the liver.

Physically:

Liver: is a large reddish brown organ that weighs about five pounds, is protected by the ribcage, lies just below the diaphragm and partly overlaps the stomach. It is a bio-chemical factory that has a number of functions, most of which concern the digestion, use and storage of the energy in food, and cleaning up the mess afterward. The liver converts the excess glucose in the bloodstream into glycogen, which is then stored until the glucose levels of the blood begin to fall. The liver then reconverts the stored glycogen into glucose to be released into the bloodstream as needed keeping the blood sugar level constant to maintain energy and build new cells. This is the fuel we use to run our body - muscles use the glycogen stored in them for energy. This is how it works - short version:

The **small intestine** breaks down the food we eat into molecules that are compatible with the blood both size wise and chemically. These molecules are taken by the blood via the portal vein up to the liver. The liver receives the nutrient rich blood, inspects, cleanses, and adjusts its composition before sending the blood back out into general circulation. The liver detoxifies any harmful substances, like drugs, alcohol, nicotine or unwanted hormones, and de-animates excess amino acids into urea to be excreted by the kidneys. The liver is a manufacturing site for enzymes, cholesterol, proteins, Vitamin A from carotene, blood coagulation factors and other elements. It destroys old red blood cells and converts the hemoglobin molecule into bilirubin, the principle pigment of bile.

The liver also takes any excess sugar molecules and converts them to fat which it stores directly around itself for use in case of famine. Fat is harder to break down and use than glycogen, but it stores longer. Liver stored glycogen is short-term, enough for about six hours. Muscle cells also store glycogen, but use it for muscular activity. Carbohydrate molecules easily convert to sugar, and alcohol is only one molecule off sugar.

The **gall bladder** simply stores bile which emulsifies fats, and we don't even think about it unless it develops gallstones, which are actually formed from cholesterol when excessive amounts are being excreted in the bile. Gallstones usually give no symptoms, but can either irritate the lining of the gallbladder or block the bile duct.

The **stomach** is simply a mixing bag for food and acids before they enter the small intestine. We don't think too much about the stomach either, unless it is empty and complaining, complaining about what you put in it, or the lining is irritated from acid or medications. Remember the nausea position is at the temples, but there is a "Church Supper Position", with your hand on your stomach, that is good for food-induced indigestion, or chronic ailments like ulcers. Stomach problems often spontaneously clear up when you are doing daily Reiki treatments on yourself.

For recent (within a few weeks) heart attack patients (not strokes, they are different) you might want to skip the breast area, especially if it causes any discomfort. The pace maker of the heart runs on energy, and sometimes the Reiki energy can feel like too much in this area. I have had feedback that immediate, direct Reiki helped heal heart muscle damage after a heart attack in one case. So, there you have it again - follow your instincts, and what the person tells you. It is never necessary to leave your hands in a position, especially if a person is in physical discomfort. The Reiki will eventually get where it needs to go and do what it needs to do no matter where you put your hands. The recipient's body will take care of that process.

Metaphysically:

Even very skinny alcoholics can have very fatty livers. Fat deposits can be the beginning of cirrhosis, which is simply the replacement of liver tissue with useless fibrous tissue. Theory #223: it is possible that the fat around the liver actually protects or muffles the memories of people and unexpressed emotion that the liver handles on an energetic level. So overuse of empty calories of carbohydrates, sugars and alcohol can actually help keep these memories in the emotional garbage can, with the fatty cover kept on tight.

Reiki energy can help release these emotions or emotional memories, without the person even having to be aware of what they are. Reiki also fills the space with a higher vibration so that the person is not feeling empty, and wanting to go out and re-experience the same emotion in order to fill the space with a familiar feeling.

The metaphysical connections for the gall bladder are pretty clear. Just roll around the words bile and gall in your mind, and you get the emotional connections - bitter, disagreeable, impudent, peevish, spiteful.

Words and language are also a vibrational energy. Pay attention to the energetic of words that you use, or your client uses in relationship to their body, mind, spirit, general health and well being. Often life attitudes and manifestation of dis-ease are concurrent. Pay attention to habitual sayings often tossed off without conscious thought. They are clues to underlying assumptions, beliefs, and attitudes about life in general and healing in particular. I personally believe in the power of consciously changing language, including the use of positive affirmations to bring to consciousness negative attitudes and beliefs. Once recognized these can be changed, reprogrammed or released. The effects can be far reaching.

Chest Position #2 - Pancreas and Spleen, Heart

Hands: Hands are in the same position as in chest position #1, simply move them gently, one hand at a time, side by side to the upper left quadrant, both hands on the ribcage below the breast over the pancreas and spleen. Or one hand above the breast more toward the upper chest, and one hand on the ribcage.

You read all about the breast earlier in *Body Attitudes/ Appropriate Touch*, so we'll just skip on ahead to the pancreas and spleen functions.

Physically: The pancreas secretes pancreatic enzymes for digestion, and insulin to regulate the uptake and use of blood sugar by the cells. If the pancreas feels cold it can indicate an insulin imbalance, or medication for same. The spleen deals with any blood diseases like leukemia or anemia.

Metaphysically: The heart chakra is about unconditional love. The solar plexus chakra is about unconditional healing. Breasts are about nurturing, especially self nurture. The pancreas is about losses in life, especially anything that was "sweet" to you - relationships, people, pets, job, house, etc.; unresolved emotion (even if I expressed it, if it is unresolved it is probably vibrationally stored in the pancreas), and unfinished business. The spleen deals with any emotional blood dis-eases: hot blood - anger, extremes of emotion; bad blood - resentments or long held grudges.

Physically:

The **pancreas** lives in the back of the abdomen behind the lower part of the stomach. In addition to producing pancreatic enzymes for digestion, it produces the hormones glucagon and insulin. Glucagon raises the level of glucose in the blood by releasing it from liver glycogen. Insulin reduces the level of glucose in the blood by encouraging it to enter the muscle and liver cells as glycogen for storage. Adrenaline "antagonizes" insulin - it overrides the effects of insulin and causes the liver and muscles to convert their stores of glycogen to glucose.

The **spleen and thymus** (head position #4) are the largest parts of the adult lymphatic system, which is an important part of our immune system. The spleen lies at the left side of the abdomen between the lower ribs and the stomach. It is a fibrous sponge filled with lymphoid tissue which filters blood as it passes through. It stores about 20% of the blood supply at any one time. It releases this blood back into circulation in case of emergency to keep the blood pressure stable. As long as it has so much of the blood at its disposal, the spleen helps keep house by destroying worn out red blood cells and making lymphocytes and antibodies.

The spleen contains phagocytes (white blood cells) which ingest the spent red blood cells and turn their hemoglobin into bilirubin and ferritin for release into blood circulation. The yellow pigment bilirubin is excreted in the bile. The protein ferritin contains the iron from the hemoglobin, and is used by the red bone marrow to make more hemoglobin.

The lymphatic system produces lymphocytes to destroy bacteria and viruses, produces antibodies, removes excess fluid from the tissues and filters any debris from it, lacteals absorb digested fat from the intestines and return it to circulation. Lymphoid tissue is formed of white cells (lymphocytes), which detect antigens and make antibodies. Lymphoid tissue occurs in lymph nodes, thymus, spleen, tonsils, adenoids, digestive tract and lungs. The lymphatic system is a bunch of lymph nodes or glands linked together by a system of tubes - lymph vessels or lymphatics. These tubes penetrate throughout the body and contain a clear fluid called lymph.

Lymph nodes contain a network of tiny passageways lined with phagocytes. About ten percent of tissue fluid flows back into the lymph capillaries instead of the bloodstream. This fluid carries the larger particles like bacteria and proteins that don't fit through the blood capillaries, and allows them to be filtered out of the body. When the bacteria, viruses, protein molecules and other particles flow by in the lymph, the phagocytes or white blood cells engulf the offenders. Antibodies are made in response to the antigens trapped by the phagocytes, hence those killer T cells we hear so much about - T is for Thymus. (And S is for Superman as we all know. Funny how the letter was placed right in this area!)

Diabetes results when the hormone producing islet cells within the pancreas fail to produce enough insulin, or when the body cells are not able to use it properly. Insulin tells the cells to take up and use the blood sugar. People with either form of diabetes, juvenile or adult onset, cannot control the level of glucose in the blood. It can rise so high that blood sugar is excreted in the urine, or fall so low that the brain cannot function and the person goes into a coma. The organs of the body cannot run well if the fuel mixture is either too rich or too lean, complications of diabetes can affect many parts of the body. You can treat diabetics in reverse order from hips to chest. It will help the circulation, which is often slowed down with this dis-ease.

Juvenile onset, or insulin dependent diabetes is the rarer form of the disease and results from the islets producing too little insulin. This can be from an inherited tendency, or triggered by a viral infection that affects the islet cells. Adult onset diabetes usually affects people over the age of forty. Their bodies are not able to use the insulin properly. This type is often able to be controlled through careful regulation of diet, and may not need insulin by tablet or injections.

Chest Position #3: Waist, Small Intestine, Transverse Colon

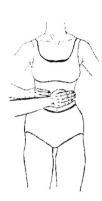

Hands: Across the waist. Fingertips of one hand on the midline, heel of the other hand on the fingertips.

Physically: Serves small intestine, which does all digestion and absorption of food, and the top part of the transverse colon, part of the large intestine.

Metaphysically: General memory. Absorption, retention and use of information.

Physically:

Intestines, digestion and absorption: physical digestion starts with chewing solid food into smaller pieces (bolus) to get it to the stomach where it is churned with acids and gastric juice with the warmth of the body to melt fats and turn it into a semi liquid state called chyme. Chemical digestion uses enzymes to break down carbohydrates into simple sugars, fats into fatty acids and glycerols, proteins into amino acids. Glucose, vitamins, minerals, and water are already small enough to be absorbed by the blood. Fiber, indigestible with human enzymes, remains unchanged.

The small intestine is 21 feet long and is a marvel of packing. I am always impressed by a good job of packing, and the small intestine is an excellent example of great packing. All 21 foot are coiled around, and held in place by ligaments so that we don't feel all the movement that is going on. The food is mixed with acid and some digestive enzymes in the stomach. The stomach then squeezes the mixed food out to travel down the length of the small intestine, being further mixed with enzymes along the way.

As the food is broken down enough to release molecules that are compatible with and capable of being carried by the blood stream, the capillaries in the villi (bumps) and microvilli (bumps on bumps) which line the small intestine absorb the molecules into the bloodstream. The nutrient rich blood goes to the liver via the portal vein for inspection and cleansing before the blood is released into general circulation. The lacteals in the villi are part of the lymphatic system. They absorb the fatty acids and glycerol, which are carried by the lymph vessels and reenter the bloodstream by the heart. The nutrients in the food are transported by the bloodstream to the cells and tissues where they are assimilated and used.

The capillary rich villi and micro-villi are finger-like projections on the inside of the small intestine (imagine a terry cloth towel). Just like West Virginia would make Texas if somebody flattened it out, the absorptive area of the small intestine equals approximately the area of a football field.

The unused material, mainly water and undigested matter such as fiber, passes from the small intestine to the large intestine. As it moves slowly along, most of the water is absorbed through the wall of the large intestine. Enormous numbers of bacteria live in the intestine and feed on the contents, producing some B vitamins, important for vegetarians, and Vitamin K which is a blood clotting factor. Waste is released from the body as feces or stool.

A lot of our blood supply is tied up in digestion at any one time, unless we are dealing with an adrenaline overload. If there is a large amount of adrenaline in the bloodstream, the breathing and heart rate are increased, and blood is diverted away from the intestines and the skin to be sent to the long muscles of the arms and legs so we can either throw a punch or run. This is the fight, flight or freeze syndrome. The suddenly redistributed blood supply can produce symptoms of feeling lightheaded, breathless, and slightly nauseous. Adrenaline also antagonizes insulin, causing the liver and muscles to convert glycogen to glucose for immediate use.

Chest Position #4 - Across the Hips

Hands: Across the hips in a straight line, fingertips of one hand on the midline, heel of the other hand on the fingertips.

Physically: Serves bladder, urinary tract, ascending and descending colon. For women it also serves ovaries and uterus, and anything systemic or hormonal, including migraines. For men it serves the bladder and prostate, as does the fourth position on the back. In pregnancy, make an additional position for the baby as soon as the baby can be felt, cupping your hands over the belly. Babies usually love Reiki.

Metaphysically: Self acceptance at a very basic level. Ki point, or hara, center of gravity for the body, center of universe for the spirit; spleen chakra - self esteem.

Physically:

Bladder - a great many chemical reactions take place within an organism to keep it alive. The products of some of these chemical reactions are poisonous and must be removed from the body. The excretory organs of the body and the products they remove are: 1. skin: water; 2. lungs: carbon dioxide and water; 3. liver: converts bilirubin into bile, and also modifies spent hormones which are secreted by kidneys; 4. kidneys: secrete urea and other nitrogenous waste. Salts not needed by the body join uric acid and urea and water in the pelvis of the kidney, and pass as urine through the ureters into the bladder. The bladder holds the urine until it is released through the urethra.

Ovaries and uterus - ovaries are two whitish oval bodies, about an inch long, that lie in the lower abdomen on either side of the uterus. Close to each ovary is the funnel shaped opening of the Fallopian tubes, which open into a wider tube, the uterus or womb which is in the lower abdomen. The cervix is a ring of muscle that closes the lower end of the uterus where it joins the vagina. The ova or egg cells are present in the ovary at the time a baby girl is born, and no more form in her lifetime (sperm are continually produced in the testes). Ovaries produce estrogen and progesterone, both of which prepare the uterus for implantation by an embryo.

Menopause occurs when the hormones of the menstrual cycle are reduced. Symptoms of hot flashes, sweats and depression can happen as a result hormone imbalance. Osteoporosis, or calcium loss from the skeletal bones, increases after menopause. There are many herbal and homeopathic remedies for menopausal symptoms. Hormone replacement therapy needs to be considered carefully.

Hormones are chemical messengers - chemical substances which are produced by endocrine glands in one part of the body and are transported by the bloodstream to affect tissues or organs in another part of the body. Although each hormone travels to all parts of the body it only affects certain cells and/or target organs.

Endocrine glands or ductless glands secrete hormones directly into the bloodstream. Exocrine glands have ducts through which secretions are removed. The pancreas, ovaries and testes have both endocrine and exocrine functions. The endocrine system is: Hypothalamus and pituitary gland (for more information see the brain section), thyroid and parathyroid (throat section), pancreas (upper left side of abdomen), adrenals (on top of kidneys, third position on the back, coming up), ovaries or testes.

Any symptoms that are systemic or hormonally based for women are treated in the fourth or hip position. When I say anything systemic or hormonal, I mean everything from PMS to pimples. Often skin problems are linked with hormone imbalance. Mrs. Takata suggested treating breast cancer from the ovary/uterus area, feeling that this is where the cancer stems from.

Migraines are treated from the hip position, especially for women. For men, treat migraines, or anything systemic or hormonal, from the coccyx area. A man's base chakra is lower than a woman's. Think about it and you will get why.

Migraines are vascular headaches and are often hormonally induced. For women, the frequency of headaches is often relieved after menopause. Migraines can also be triggered by food allergies. There are some good books on the subject. In general, avoid nicotine, caffeine, chocolate, aged cheeses, preserved foods like pickles and sausages, monosodium glutamate, alcohol - especially red wine, champagne, dark or heavy drinks, white sugar, salt, nuts, yeast products. The good news is, sex is good for getting rid of migraines. Unless the person you are having sex with gives you a headache, of course.

Food allergies can cause a lot of problems we don't fully recognize, and our tendency is to actually crave things we are allergic to. The is because of a phenomena called the histamine reaction. Here is how it works: If I eat cheese, and the protein molecules are too large for the bloodstream but get in there anyway, they can irritate all my cells, since the blood goes to all my cells. The cells react by swelling slightly - a histamine reaction.

For example: if I eat cheese every day for a few years, my cells become used to the histamine reaction, and come to think of it as normal. If I quit eating cheese for a week, the cells will go back to and remain the size they are intended to be. But they will be unhappy, because they have become used to their slightly swollen size and think that is normal.

So my body will go through withdrawal symptoms that can include getting a headache, until my body readjusts itself to the "new" normal, which is actually the original normal that got reprogrammed. Then I'll really notice a reaction if I eat a piece of cheese, because my body is now clear, and will tell me right away that I have put an allergen in it.

Multiple allergies are sometimes hard to trace, but worth looking for. That is why sometimes a food will cause a problem and sometimes not. It works this way: a person can be more allergic to aged cheeses in the spring when the pollen count is high. Or a martini will trigger a headache if the person eats salted nuts with it, but won't trigger a headache if they don't eat salted nuts. Sounds crazy, but it is true.

Metaphysically:

Even if the uterus and/or ovaries have been surgically removed, the energetic of the organs is still there. Remember Kirlian photography, and how it will pick up the entire energetic body of a leaf, even if part of the leaf is missing. Each cell in our body has the blueprint of us in our perfection in the DNA and RNA. So each cell contains a hologram of a complete body. Reiki treats all the bodies - spiritual or etheric, energetic and physical - it is important to treat the body as if it were whole.

There is another thing about hysterectomies. Not all physicians or surgeons are compassionate about a woman's loss of the parts that biologically define her as female. And perhaps the woman herself may have been influenced by the somewhat cavalier attitude that used to prevail about this surgery. At one time it was the most commonly performed elective or unnecessary surgery. A lot of women have not done the actual body mourning that takes place after a surgery which removes a part of the whole, even if that part was not functioning properly. There can be a lot of scar tissue, both physical and emotional, in this area.

This hip position also covers the general area for self-esteem and self-acceptance. It is the area of the spleen chakra, which deals with passion. A lot of people confuse this with sex. It is nice when sex is passionate, however, this is not the only definition of passion. I can be passionate about life, painting, causes, politics (not me in particular, but some people get that way), people, healing - lots of things.

The base chakra is about being alive. Passion in the spleen chakra is more like, "How do you feel about being alive?" So - how do I feel about being who I am? In the case of a woman, working over the ovaries and uterus, it can be how do you feel about being who you are as a female person? This is self acceptance at a very basic level.

BACK POSITIONS

General Information

For the head and chest positions, the client was lying on their back, face up. After we finish the chest positions and any auxiliary positions we might add, we ask the client to turn over, and lie on their stomach. If the client cannot lie comfortably on their stomach, perhaps because of a colostomy, recent surgery, advanced pregnancy, back or other problem, they can lie on their side. This will give you access to the area. If they cannot lie on their side, you can slip your hands under the back and work the positions from there. If I have to accommodate in this way, I usually do the back positions along with the chest positions, one hand on top of and the other hand under the body.

Draw an imaginary line down the center of the back. All positions are worked from the center line here as well as on the chest, no matter the size of the person. If you work from the center line you are sure of covering the organs and glands.

There are three major muscle groups covering the back. These are:

The trapezius muscle is a sheet of muscle that begins at the neck, goes to about the center of the shoulder blades, covers lots of smaller muscles and helps hold the arms on the body.

The latissimus dorsi covers the mid-back and ribcage, supports the ribs, helps keep them together and basically keeps your guts from falling out.

The gluteus maximus covers the tail-bone and keeps your legs attached to the body.

There are thirty one pairs of spinal nerves that come off the spine and deal with musculature and movement. We already dealt with the twelve pairs of cranial nerves that take care of our senses and organs when we treated the head.

So, anyplace you put your hands on the back, you are treating about one third of the musculature and a few pairs of nerves.

You have probably spent about an hour treating the body by this time (or about ten hours reading this book, unless you just skipped to the good parts). So the back positions will seem to go faster. The body is used to the rhythm of your touch, and is probably sucking up the Reiki in a steady draw.

<u>Back Position #1:</u>   Shoulders

<u>Hands:</u> across the tops of the shoulders, high up on the rounded part, fingertips on the midline, heel of the other hand on the fingertips.

<u>Physically:</u> relaxes shoulder muscles, relieves stress and tension

<u>Metaphysically:</u> burdens, responsibilities, things we have shouldered or taken on are treated (and released) in this position.

People who tend to perceive the world visually may carry their shoulders up around their ears. I always thought this was a normal position and posture. I simply thought I had a short neck. I still have to remind myself to straighten my back and lower my shoulders, and allow my neck to be seen. I have come to understand this position as being "wrapped tight". I am never accused of being wrapped too tight in other areas of my being, but I often am here. I recognize it immediately when I see it in others.

This area of the shoulders is where a person could carry a yoke. Yokes were used to carry buckets for transporting material easily. Sometimes I imagine I have one of these yokes with buckets attached, which hold things I have taken on in my life. Since I am an inveterate collector, I can imagine that I may have collected a few responsibilities that aren't really mine. Every once in a while, I like to dump out the buckets and see what is in them. Do I really need everything there? Or anything there? It is like dumping out my purse to see what I've collected, or what had bred in the dark while I wasn't looking. Sometimes I even take a yoke holiday, and step out of the entire apparatus and walk around without it for awhile.

I used to work as an assistant to a photographer, Robin Quinn. In the morning we would pack for a shoot. Each piece of camera equipment was chosen with care. At the end of the day, even a one pound lens would weigh five pounds, or at least it seemed that way.

More and more I try to take the same care in selecting the responsibilities in my life as I used to do with my photographic equipment. Just because it is there doesn't mean I have to take it along. Do I need it? Is it useful? Will it serve me? Louise Hay states that we aren't meant to carry burdens. Our responsibilities are meant to be joys. I like that idea. Can I accept and handle my responsibilities with joy?

Lately, I have been paying more attention to the feelings I have when I agree to do something. Does it feel like a burden or a joy? Whichever way, it is usually the same feeling that will stay with me as I carry it along. And if I hear the words, "I have no choice.", I stop what I am doing and find at least six other choices. I don't have to like them, I just want to register that I always have a choice.

Back Position #2: Adrenals

Hands: Just below the shoulder blades, forming a straight line as in position #1, fingertips of one hand on midline, heel of the hand on the fingertips.

Physically: Adrenal glands give us adrenaline, and cortisone, an anti-inflammatory hormone that is important for managing chronic pain.

Metaphysically: Serves extremes of emotion, overwork, shock, trauma, extremes of emotion. Adrenaline cycle is thought to be a basis for addictions.

Physically:

Adrenal glands are triangular shaped and are attached to the back of the abdominal cavity. They are surrounded by fat, and sit on top of the kidneys. They are made up of an outer layer, the adrenal cortex, that produces hormones called corticosteroids. Corticosteroids help to control the metabolism of fats, carbohydrates, and proteins; and help to maintain a balance of salts and water, which helps control blood pressure, and reduces inflammation and pain, as in arthritis. The inner zone is the adrenal medulla, it has nerve connections to the brain and produces adrenaline.

The brain responds to stress by sending nerve impulses to the adrenal medulla to release adrenaline into the blood. Adrenaline affects a number of organs and functions: it increases the heartbeat, causes the breathing to become faster and deeper to increase oxygenation of the blood and promote rapid removal of carbon dioxide; constricts the arterioles in the skin and digestive system to direct more blood to the long muscles of body; tenses the muscles of the body so they are ready to respond; causes the liver to convert glycogen to glucose for immediate use; begins conversion of fats to fatty acids in blood for muscle contraction. Adrenaline is converted to a less active compound by the liver, which is then excreted by the kidneys. Caffeine, nicotine, or any drug with *-ine* stimulates the adrenals, as do shock and trauma.

Adrenaline reaction is one of our natural defenses. When we had to run from the saber-toothed tigers, it was a real necessity. An adrenaline reaction bypasses conscious thought – a sort of "Move it or lose it now!" as opposed to an intellectual debate about the pros and cons of possible courses of action. And the physical activity of running from the saber-toothed tiger helped to metabolize the adrenaline. However, many stressful situations today do not require physical activity. So we can be left with an overload of adrenaline in our system that can leave us feeling tense and anxious, or even exhausted when the adrenals have been overworked.

The adrenaline cycle also triggers the release of endorphins in the brain, which are our natural opiates, or pain killers. They feel good.

There is a theory that addictions, whether behavioral or substance, are based on the adrenaline/endorphin cycle. In one experiment, when gamblers were tested with portable bio-feedback equipment, it was noted that the physiological changes in their bodies happened before anybody thought they would. The changes did not start when the gamblers went to the track, or placed the bet, with the amount of money bet, or even with winning or losing. The most physiological changes occurred when the gambler *thought* about going to the track. The physiological effects began and were maintained with thought, which triggered the adrenaline reaction. Treating the adrenals may help break an addiction cycle.

Mark Twain once observed that humans are the only animals who blush – or need to. This concept fascinates me – that the body has such strong and immediate physiological reactions to our thoughts. How important to our physical health and well being our thought processes can be.

Back Position #3: Kidneys

Hands: across the back, just above the waist, fingertips on the midline, heel of the hand on the fingertips

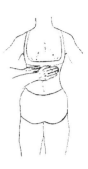

Physically: Serves the kidneys which filter and clean the blood

Metaphysically: angers and resentments, chronic "piss-offedness"

Physically:

The kidneys are bean shaped, red-brown structures that are encased in a tough transparent membrane, embedded in perirenal fat and attached to the back of the abdominal wall behind the peritoneum at the level of the twelfth thoracic to third lumbar vertebrae. The right kidney is usually lower than the left because of the liver. The renal artery branches off the aorta and brings oxygenated blood to the kidneys, the renal vein carries deoxygenated blood to the vena cava, the ureter runs from each kidney carrying urine to the bladder in the lower part of the abdomen.

About one pint of blood passes through the kidneys every minute, and is filtered under very high pressure by about a million nephrons (tubules) in each kidney - a total of about 180 liters of liquid per day. Their function is to filter substances out of the blood, remove the unwanted substances such as urine, and selectively re-absorb wanted substances back into the blood. During this process they monitor the salt and mineral content of the blood, balance blood pressure, check the viscosity and fluid content of the blood. They kidneys are so efficient that the body can function with only one when necessary.

Kidneys are affected by medication, alcohol and drug use. You can sometimes feel signs or effects of medication, alcohol or drug use while giving a Reiki treatment. Even overuse of over the counter drugs like aspirin or non-aspirin substitutes can cause the kidneys to feel irritated or even inflamed. Renal colic is severe pain in the small of the back and diagonally around to the front of the abdomen caused by a kidney stone which has left the kidney and is passing down the ureter.

Metaphysically:

As with the spleen, the kidneys deal with metaphysical blood diseases: hot blood, bad blood, angers and resentments. Chronic piss-offedness is a general attitude of "Nothing is ever right or ever will be so let me just grump my way through life and make everyone I come in contact with as miserable as I am or at the very least extremely aware of my misery." Sort of the antithesis of an attitude of gratitude.

Back Position #4: Sacrum and Coccyx

Hands: Hands together at the base of the spine. Or, "cheek to cheek" - fingertips at the midline on the coccyx, lay hands down over one side, heel of hands on coccyx for other side.

Physically: Serves spinal column and any male hormonal imbalance.

Metaphysically: Any kind of abuse: physical, spiritual, sexual, emotional, verbal, as well as any associated humiliation, guilt or shame reactions.

Physically:

The backbone or spine is a column of thirty-three small bones called vertebrae. The top twenty four are separate bones, the next five are fused to form the sacrum, the next four form the coccyx, which is a remnant of a tail. The backbone is held in a natural S-shaped by the muscles of the back and the ligaments that link the vertebrae. The backbone is protected from damage by jarring because the cartilage discs between the vertebrae act as shock absorbers, and the shape of the spine makes it behave like a spring.

The vertebrae column supports the upper part of the body, encloses and protects the spinal cord, provides points of attachment for the ribs and the muscles of the back, allows movement of the head and the trunk. The joint between the skull and the top vertebrae (atlas) allows the head to move forwards and backwards. The joint between the first and second vertebrae (atlas and axis) allows the head to turn from side to side.

The spinal cord is firmly attached to the second sacral vertebrae, and the meninges that hold the spinal fluid come out of the spinal column and form the coccyx. So every joke you ever heard about sitting on your brains has an element of truth. Anything that has ever happened to you in this area has registered vibrationally here and in the brain, and can be treated here.

Metaphysically:

Basically, there are five types of abuse: emotional/mental, verbal, physical, sexual and spiritual. Each of these begins as a thought form or attitude, then can move to a verbal level, then to a physical level. Spiritual abuse is something like, "I am God and you are not," or I have access to God and you do not, therefore…" in reference to a person (guru-type) or an institution.

Auxiliary Back Positions:

Balance position - one hand on coccyx, one hand at top of the spine

Fingers pointed down over coccyx, other hand across fingertips - base chakra, good for depression or hemorrhoids.

Backs of knees if you did the fronts

Bottoms of feet

To finish the treatment you can, clear or "wipe down" the aura – move your hands several times down the back an inch or two above the body. I think of this as clearing anything that has come up in the treatment.

Mrs. Takata finished treatments by "raking" the back – firmly drawing the fingers down the length of the back on either side of the spinal column several times to "wake up the body".

There is some legal concern in some states re: "manipulation of the body for profit." (Don't you just love that phrase?) This means to lay hands on the body in a quiet manner is one thing, to manipulate the body in any way (i.e. massage) can require state-approved training and licensing. Use your good judgment here as you practice. Sometimes I do the more physical ending, and tell people "This part is free."

Then I gently remove the blanket. Usually this movement encourages the person to wake up if they have been asleep. I give them a few minutes to get up slowly. Then they can get off the table and sit in a chair.

I offer them a drink of water or a cup of tea. They need a few minutes to come to themselves, they may have been asleep, or in an altered state, meaning deeply relaxed like a long meditation. I may also feel like I have been in a long meditation. If I have been doing a house call, I take the time to go to the bathroom and wash my hands before I leave, if possible. I'm usually pretty together by the time I fold up any blankets, or a table if I brought one. I remind people (including myself) to be alert driving home, and just for today everyone else has the right of way as reaction time can be a bit slower than usual.

Meditation on the Reiki Healing Principles - Five Precepts

The Japanese language is one of the picture languages. Since the characters are actually picture representations of concepts or things, there can be many word interpretations of the same characters or combinations of characters. Somewhere in each language interpretation is the essence of the representation and its meaning.

That is why there are many translations/interpretations of the precepts or principles - beginning right here with the name of them. Some Masters call these Spiritual Precepts, some call them the Reiki Healing Principles. Usui called them the Five Precepts. A calligraphy used by Usui has recently been discovered. This translation is in **bold.** I will give the translation used by Takata in ***bold italics***. The translation I like and use follows in regular print. I also outline how I interpret and experience the precepts in my life. Today. Understanding evolves and deepens with practice.

The order of the precepts is different from different sources. Usui listed them as:

1. **Today, feel no anger.**
2. **Have no worries.**
3. **Feel gratitude.**
4. **Show diligence in your undertakings.**
5. **Treat others with kindness.**

These Precepts are a part of the story of Usui's journey, a part of his learning about physical and spiritual healing. In this part of the story we find him in the beggar's camp, after several years of healing work with the beggars. He speaks to one of the first beggars he healed, and helped to get a new name and job in order to start a new life. Usui finds out that the beggar has returned to his old way of life even though his physical ailment remains healed. Usui can't understand why. The beggar explains that he didn't like regular work, it was repetitive and hard, and didn't pay much. Begging was easier, and more to his taste. Usui is confused and hurt, and goes back to his hut to meditate, asking for understanding.

Usui realized he made a monumental assumption that the beggars were only beggars because they were physically handicapped or ill. He thought that if they were physically healed, they would automatically want to lead a "better" life - the life of "an honorable citizen", having a regular job, paying taxes and all that. He found out otherwise. Usui found that even when physically well, the beggar's basic value system differed from Usui's own, and that the value system didn't automatically heal and grow the way Usui thought it would, or should - namely by becoming congruent with his.

Usui remembered back to the time he became a monk. He applied to monastery after monastery, explaining that he wanted to study the phenomena of physical healing. And time after time was told that spiritual healing was the most important. Heal the spirit and the body will follow.

One thing Usui discovered was that both aspects were equally important, both physical and spiritual healing. And an intellectual understanding would also be useful, bringing the mind and emotions into the equation.

Usui then came up with five spiritual healing principles that a person can practice and live each day, bringing healing to all areas of life. As he thought through each one, he understood some things about the way he was living his life, about his own right work in the world.

Usui understood that he was offering a gift to people who hadn't really asked for it. He understood that his agenda, his unspoken bargain, was to impose his beliefs and value system on the beggars instead of honoring their way of life as it was. This was not an honest exchange. He was coming from a place of knowing or being "better than" in his own mind.

Here he understood that his right work was teaching people who want to learn how to heal themselves and each other, not healing people who didn't really want to be healed, or trying to change their way of living and being.

And so he left the beggar's community and became again what he started out as - a teacher. This time he is a teacher of Reiki. He is teaching a system of healing that anyone who wants to can learn to heal themselves and each other. He thanked the beggars all for the lessons and the learning, for truly being his teacher. He honors them and their integrity, and himself and his integrity. And he moves on.

1. **Today, feel no anger.** *Just for today, do not anger.* Just for today, I release all anger.

This one is about expectations, and control, and being human. At every minute, we have free choice in our lives. We can decide to go this way or that, do this thing or not. We have choice about our actions and reactions.

When I feel anger, it is most often connected to the words "righteous" and "frustrated". I am holding an expectation that was not met, either consciously or unconsciously. If it is a righteous anger, then someone has not met an expectation that I assumed was a moral or ethical guide for both of us. Frustrated is usually about expectations based on an agreement or contract, conscious/spoken or not.

As I have worked with this principle, I've found that a lot of my contracts were actually unspoken bargains. "I do this for you, and I just know you will do that for me." I've come to be wary of unspoken bargains, and am much better at spotting them coming either way, either from me to another or from another to me. I am also better at making clear contracts, voicing my expectations instead of assuming the other person knows what I want and is both capable of and willing to provide it.

In any case, I have a choice about what to do with my anger. I can feel it, acknowledge it, and release it so I can speak clearly to the person about what I am feeling and why. This way, I can possibly get some clear information that I can use as a basis for a decision on the subject, or the future direction of our relationship. Or I can keep my anger, let it smolder, let it fuel resentment and misunderstanding, let it cloud the rest of my feelings and actions for however long it takes to go away, or to explode and affect whomever happens to be in the way. It is totally my choice.

So, it is OK to feel anger. That is just a signal to say that something is out of order and needs my attention. I treat anger like an acid. Since I am the one experiencing it, it can burn me first, especially if I do not handle it carefully. If I am acting from anger, I am probably not making clear choices. "You leave me no other choice!" is usually a warning thought for me. If I hear this in my mind, I'm sure of at least two things. First that I am angry, and second that this is not a true statement. I always have choices. I just may not like them. I do need to examine them, though.

I find it helpful to use Reiki to support living this principle. I imagine myself and my relationship to the person/situation I am having difficulty with like a hologram in my hand. I surround this image with Reiki, ask for wisdom and enlightenment on the situation, and the ability to receive and act on these with grace; say my forgiveness and release affirmations; activate the divine within myself and within the situation; ask for the highest possible solution (it will come if I ask for it); and let some time pass before I act on any situation I am angry about.

2. **Have no worries.** *Just for today, do not worry.* Just for today, I release all worry.

This one is about trust. Just for today, I trust in the Universe to provide me with all that I need, just as it provides me with the air that I breathe. I trust that the divine is at work in myself and in each situation for the highest good of all concerned. I release my need to direct the process or to control the outcome. I honor the path of every living thing, including my own. I simply bless the divine within each person and situation, ask for and accept wisdom to guide me in my choices and on my path. I gratefully accept all blessings set in store for me, "lessons" included, even those I don't think I want or need, or understand yet. I trust that they are a part of a greater picture that the Universe designs, incorporating my decisions and choices along with everyone else's. I trust that the "Universe is unfolding as it should."

A Reiki Master named Paul Mitchell taught me a lot about this principle in an Aikido workshop. We were working with swords. A lot of the ladies were flinching. They were worried that they would either get hit themselves, or that they might inflict pain on another. Paul was trying to teach us all that we can take care of ourselves if we choose to. He said, "Whether you flinch or whether you don't flinch, the result is the same. So, don't flinch!" He meant for us to keep our eyes open and our wits about us, to practice taking care of ourselves as we were taught in this exercise, and to trust that others can and will take care of themselves if we let them. Actually the best gift we can give another person is our conscious attention and our best shot. A good thing to remember in the helping professions.

How simple. All the times I have gotten hit with something simply because I refused to look at the situation and make a clear choice about what to do. And all the times I have ended up hurting another because I was trying to take care of them or fix things for them instead of just being present, encouraging them to take care of themselves and do their own healing. When I come from a place of openness, I can choose how to take care of myself. I can release all worry, and any flinching.

Two affirmations follow that I use to help me release both anger and worry, adapted from Catherine Ponder's "The Dynamic Laws of Prosperity".

I forgive and release absolutely everyone and everything in my life that can possibly need forgiveness and release, including myself, in body mind and spirit, in life, work and surroundings, in all time space and dimension. I am free and you are free. I release you in love and fill these spaces with unconditional love.

I bless you and I bless you for the goodness of God that is at work in and through you as it is in and through me. I claim for you as I claim for myself that the goodness of God is all that exists in this situation, and all else is now and forevermore dissolved. I am free and you are free. I release you in love, and fill these spaces with unconditional love.

3. **Feel gratitude.** *Show gratitude to every living thing.* I shall show gratitude for all my many blessings, or, I shall live an attitude of gratitude.

Gratitude signals acceptance. This works on all levels, and for all kinds of blessings, including life lessons. I have this theory I call spiral up or spiral down. Nothing stays static, and a body in motion tends to stay in motion in the same general direction. If I am giving my attention to gratitude, then I am not available to run my control dramas, or emphasize the things or situations that have not met my standards or expectations. If I am using my energy to say thank you, and perhaps adding what else I might like, then I am not using my energy to complain, be resentful, or find more things that are wrong.

If I am grateful for the blessings I receive, the Universe will give me more. If I am ungrateful, or ignore them, the Universe will say, "She doesn't want any, good - we'll give it to somebody else, somebody with more gratitude, more enthusiasm."

So I make sure I thank the Universe for all my many blessings, especially the small ones. If I love and cherish the small ones, isn't the Universe more likely to trust me with the big ones? If I am ungrateful or oblivious to my small blessings, will the Universe want to give me more of what I am ignoring or taking for granted?

Another level is: I cannot change something I do not own. So, a friend may give me a gift (like an observation about my behavior or actions). At first I may not know, or even think, I want this gift. If I do not first accept the gift of this observation, accept that is so (if it is), if I don't "own" the behavior, I cannot change the behavior.

It is like this: Aunt Maude gives me a sweater for Christmas. It doesn't fit, and I intend to take it back to the store, and exchange it for one that does fit. But somehow, in the holiday confusion, it gets put away in the Christmas boxes. I lose awareness of its existence. Somebody either reminds me, or comes across the sweater later on. I am now aware of it, I "own" it, and I can do something about it.

4. **Show diligence in your undertakings.** *Earn your living honestly.* I shall earn my living with integrity.

I looked honesty and integrity up in . *The Collins Paperback English Dictionary.*

Honest: "1. trustworthy; 2. genuine; 3. just or fair; characterized by sincerity; 5. without pretensions; 6. respectable." *Integrity:* "1. adherence to moral principles, honesty; 2. the quality of soundness, of being unimpaired; 3. unity, wholeness."

The concept of genuine says the most to me. There is this difference between efficient and effective - efficient is doing the job right, effective is doing the right job. I like to think of integrity as knowing and being congruent with my right work in the world (effectiveness) and then doing it joyfully and well (efficiency).

There is also a quality of rightness and joy when I am doing my right work with integrity. If the joy is not present, even if I am peeling potatoes or doing paperwork, something is off - I am out of integrity with either myself or my work, I am simply not doing the right job, or the right job at the right time. If I quiet my mind, my joyful reaction will signal my right work for this moment in time or time in my life.

Knowing right work is important. I imagine that when Usui decided to leave teaching and become a student, leave formal schooling and become a monk, leave and become a healer, and then when he decided to leave the beggars community and become a teacher again he knew what his right work was. For me, it took time for the transition, but I knew when my right work was teaching Reiki, and all the steps I took in that direction had the quality of joy, even when they were difficult.

If I honor everyone's path, I can allow for everyone to be in their right work. Even if I don't see the value of it myself, I trust that value is there. Usui allowed that the beggars have their place, too. They provide a place for others to give. Their job is to receive. They are part of the balance of the world. We are each an expression of the Divine mind, with our own talents and potentials. We are all in service to each other. So our work is unique and blessed, no matter what we choose to do. If we were all trumpet players, who would make the bread? And if we were all bakers, who would make the music?

Does a choice or decision feel right and joyful? Do you love what you do? If not, you could use Reiki to ask for guidance and enlightenment, to receive that guidance when it comes, and to act on it in the highest possible manner. For myself, I may not be able to see the entire path clearly, this I know. So, I open my mind and heart, ask for divine guidance, and know that light will shine on at least the next two steps. I can take at least these next two steps if I can trust that divine guidance is at work, can see the whole pattern, and knows how these steps fit.

5. Treat others with kindness. *Honor your Parents, Teachers and Elders.* I shall honor every living thing.

I looked the word honor up in *The Collins Paperback English Dictionary*, 1988 version. It said: "1. personal integrity, allegiance to moral principles; 2. fame or glory; 3. great respect or esteem, or an outward sign of this; 4. high or noble rank; 5. a privilege or pleasure, as in *it is an honor to serve you*; 6. a woman's chastity; 7.card tricks in Bridge or Whist, 8. teeing off first in golf; 9. **do the honors** as in serving as host or hostess, or carve the meat for dinner; 10. **honor bound** as in a moral obligation; 11. **in honor of**, out of respect for; 12. **on one's honor**, on the pledge of one's word or good name; 13. to hold in respect; 14. to show courteous behavior towards; 15. to worship; 16. to confer a distinction upon; 17. to accept and then pay when due, as in a check or draft; 18. to bow or curtsy, as in dancing partner, 18. a title of certain judges."

Honoring seems to be more than "live and let live", a bit more than respect. It contains some feeling of everything the dictionary said. I may not know exactly what it is, but -

I know what it is not. It is not agreement. I can honor someone I disagree with. A friend once accused me of not hearing him. I explained, "I hear you just fine. I even understand what you are saying. I simply don't agree with you. To hear and understand what you say does not automatically lead me to agree with your point of view. In this particular case, it has the opposite effect. And that is OK."

As a Mother, I have to honor my children's paths. I don't have to agree with the decisions they make, or like them. I do have to honor them. It is their path and they must walk it.

And I remember in Usui's story, how I imagine he decides to honor his own path as well as everyone else's. He honors himself by choosing to do his right work. He honors the beggars by leaving them to walk their own path, without his judgments or interference.

As a student, I honor my teacher's experience. I know that if Linda Keiser Mardis had not chosen to honor her inner truth and walk her path with integrity, I wouldn't be typing this page today. I wouldn't be here. I know if Usui had not chosen to honor his quest and shine his particular light, Linda wouldn't have found her way, and couldn't have shone her light to help me find mine. I also honor the experience of each student who comes to me. They are my teachers, too, each in their own way. I honor all my teachers.

If You Are Considering Mastery
(Finding a Teaching Master)

Since I began practicing Reiki in the spring of 1985, many thing have happened. At that time, Reiki was an oral tradition. Nothing had been written about it in the lineage I come through. Reiki at the first level was passed on from a Master to a student in a training situation where the student was supported by hearing the history, being initiated, learning and practicing the hand positions over a three to four day period of time. The second level contained three symbols and practice in their uses. Reiki II was offered at least a hundred days after Reiki I, to allow time for the student to practice and integrate the first level. This process happened under the care and guidance of the teaching Master.

Mastery was a calling to teach, and a highly individual path. Masters became Masters through their practice, through extensive training, and in relationship with an initiated Master in the lineage of Hawayo Takata. These Masters earned their living by and dedicated their life to teaching Reiki, the Usui System of Natural Healing. Mastery was understood as a practice, a discipline, a way of life - not something arrived at like a goal, and not a credential, title, or certification.

In the Japanese culture, certain things about a tradition such as Reiki, the Usui System of Natural Healing, are understood. Transplanted into a Western culture, filtered through a different framework, a different set of values and expectations, we often do not, can not know what actually gets lost in the translation. We do know the form of the Usui System of Natural Healing as passed on by Mrs. Takata got somewhat bent in some places since Mrs. Takata died in 1980.

This bending of the form, practice, discipline was actually one of Dr. Hayashi's concerns for the Usui System if he should decide to let Mrs. Takata bring it to America. Mrs. Takata always instructed her students to practice the form she gave them as she gave it to them, and then they would know - they would understand what Reiki is through practice and experience.

In our age of information, where there better be a logical reason for everything, and spiritual practice is often something confined to a fraction of our lives instead of being incorporated into the whole of it, students are sometimes not patient enough to "understand" through long years of practice. Some want to know the "Why?" of things, and they want to know right now. Why is the form so important? After all, it wasn't written, only oral, passed on in classes. Can it be changed? If so, where can it be changed, and how, and how much? Western curiosity - let's take it apart and see how it works. Let's change this or that aspect and see what happens.

How much can be changed and still have a recognizable result? Let's test it. Maybe this can be done faster, easier, better, and especially - cheaper. For some, practice of the form moved from a discipline to a theory. Fear and competition confused things. Some Masters began to stretch and bend the form, especially in those stretchable and bendable areas of time and money.

One problem here was some difference of opinion as to the real object of the teachings in the first place. Those enamored of titles and credentials were impressed with how easy these seemed when personal practice was not emphasized, and who would know if one practiced or not? Personal expression within the form slid into changes in the form, sometimes unconsciously, sometimes consciously imposed, good intentions or not. And some of the real consequences of changes in the form were not readily apparent. Results were only recognized after some time of doing things that way. The original form by then lost or obscured, changes got perpetuated from generation to generation.

Those Masters changing the form often did not change the name of what they practiced, so it seemed the Usui System grew new definitions of itself with every passing day.

The Westernization of Reiki began to take place. Convenience and accessibility became priorities instead of just considerations. The Usui System became another weekend workshop, another tool, another easy credential in the New Age alternative therapy forest. In some new forms the emphasis on personal, daily practice got lost along the way. The path of a Master got reduced to the pursuit of a title that could easily be obtained in a few hours, for little or no commitment, financial or otherwise. The McDonald's of Reiki began to appear, complete with the assembly line, but without the quality control. The experience of a Reiki training was no longer predictable, and often unsatisfactory.

We've lost a lot along the way. Let's go back to the beginning. Let's look at practicing the form. We need a bridge. Western culture calls for a more intellectual, verbal knowledge and understanding of the Usui System and its form. We need words to explain some of the "understoods", some of the givens of an Eastern culture.

Definition is a good thing for people of a Western culture who are practicing a discipline from an Eastern culture. Although we can never be Eastern, we are beginning to understand the importance of the original instruction to keep the teachings intact, passed on from Dr. Usui to his initiates, including Dr. Hayashi; from Dr. Hayashi to his initiates including Mrs. Takata; from Mrs. Takata to her initiates, and down the line to us. They understood what this meant, we are learning.

We are beginning to understand the wisdom and necessity of daily personal practice, of putting the same things in, of maintaining the original recipe if we want the same predictable results. We are beginning to understand the dance of relationship - of essence within the container of form, of personal expression within the practice of the form.

It is now becoming clear how important the energetic of a Master is in the transmission of the Usui System of Natural Healing. Oral tradition is not simply verbal. It is an experience. It is the difference between reading a play and taking part in the performance, between observing a waltz and dancing to music. A student at any level actually embodies the practice, especially so in Mastery. This is not just knowing something in your head. It is understanding it with your heart, incorporating it in your body, and being touched in your soul.

Mrs. Takata initiated 22 Masters before her death in 1980. By 1990, through continued changes in the form, an explosion in the Reiki world population took place. Before this time, Masters observed a long period of training and discernment before initiation, and another long period of practice and discernment before taking on the responsibility of training and initiating Masters if they felt so called. From under three hundred Masters before 1985, thousands populate almost every country in the world. From several thousand students, there are now estimated a million just in Germany - one percent of the population. Reiki is on every continent and in almost every country.

And Mastery, once understood as a call that required training and strong commitments to the form of the Usui System as taught by Mrs. Takata here in the west, is now available - in some forms of Reiki - over a weekend with almost no training, practice or commitment at all. The generations between some Masters are measured in days rather than years.

So, what to do? How can you know if a Master is trained or simply initiated? What form they actually practice, since the names are confusing, and even the Master in question may not know their own history? How do you know what you are getting?

First, if you are looking for a teaching Master at any level, especially if you are considering Mastery, look around. Take your time. Read. A lot is written now, find what is worth reading. Ask questions. Sit in on classes. Pay for the privilege. It is part of honoring the teacher, part of making a clear energy exchange, part of feeling free to make other choices. At the very least, get a Reiki treatment from the Master to see if there is any energy compatibility at all. What specific form do they practice? How does it feel? What is the history? How long have they been teaching? By whom were they initiated? What does that mean to them? How is their relationship with their initiating Master?

This is a lifetime relationship, what qualities do you want? How is the communication? This is one of those decisions that affects your life, and cannot be undone. You cannot be re-initiated for the first time, if you find later that you have chosen hastily, unwisely, through ignorance, assumptions or unresolved issues. It is simply a part of your path. Reiki Mastery is a symbol, reflection, and extension of your mastery in your life.

Second, although no one could possibly keep track of what each twig on the branches of Reiki is doing, the essence of the Usui System of Natural Healing still exists, and can be used as a measure. Now new information on the history of the system is coming to light. Elder Masters who have attended to their practice over the years are sharing their wisdom and understanding of the form. The Usui System has always emphasized personal practice and experience, following the guidance of inner wisdom and knowing to the best of one's ability, honoring individual understanding and truth within the form of practice.

This element of individual practice in order to understand has been a basis for the reluctance to try to capture, and the impossibility of trying to contain the form of the Usui System in words. The elements of the form of the Usui System as generally agreed upon by Masters who practice the System, and there are exceptions, are as follows:

Elements of the Form of The Usui System of Natural Healing - Reiki

Precepts: there are five Reiki healing precepts or principles (Translation from Usui's notes).

Healing Principles

Today, feel no anger.
Have no worries.
Feel gratitude.
Show diligence in your undertakings.
Treat others with kindness.

Treatments: formal treatments follow a prescribed form, three sections, four positions in each section, approximately five minutes of Reiki in each position.

Symbols: three symbols are given in the second degree.

Initiations: there are four separate initiations in the first degree, one initiation in the second, and one initiation for Master level.

Oral tradition: there is a relationship with a Master in order to learn the system.

Form of teaching: four two to three hour sections over a two to four day period for a first degree class; minimum of 100 days practice between Reiki I and II; suggested minimum of three years practice and training between Reiki I and Mastery; suggested minimum of five to six years teaching/practice before considering training another Master, if called to take on that responsibility.

History: the story of Reiki is shared at each first level class.

Money: is a part of the form, and signifies commitment along with time, energy and practice. Fees may vary by country and sometimes by circumstance, energy exchange means an exchange of time and/or effort commensurate with the monetary fee. First level is $150 minimum, second level is $500, Master is $10,000.

Of course I feel that the path of the Usui System of Natural Healing as described by this form is the absolute best. It is the one I choose to live and work within, to teach and share. I feel that Mastery is a lifetime commitment, and needs to be considered carefully. I also recognize that there are other forms of Reiki that are just as valid to other Masters.

So- when someone asks to become a Master Candidate with me, I start by asking them three questions:

Is this your path? Is this your time? Am I the Master you wish to study with?

The answer to each question must be an unconditional, "Yes!", said and received with joy. Otherwise, we will be wasting each other's time.

This isn't about any one part of the form. And it really isn't about money. If this is your path and time, then the decision has already been made in some higher realm, and the money will be provided. The test will probably be if you can trust enough to actually receive it, and then to use it for the stated purpose. One man told me that if he had the $10,000 in his hand, and no other place to put it, he would not give it to me in exchange for his initiation. I answered his question - I was not about to bend the form to fit his needs. He answered my question - this was not his path. He found a form more compatible with his beliefs. We were both greatly relieved. We are still good friends.

The more I practice this system, the more I understand that Mastery is a lifetime commitment, it is a path, not a goal; it is lived, not arrived at like a destination. It is also not a certification or credential. Mastery is not conferred by and could not be guaranteed by any training or initiation. The initiation only acknowledges a commitment made at some higher level to be lived and practiced on this plane. That I use the term Master only means that I have the privilege and responsibility of practicing Reiki in my life on a daily basis: doing self treatment, treating others, incorporating the Reiki healing principles to the best of my ability, teaching classes and, for me, working with others who are on the path of Mastery.

Mastery is indeed an individual journey. Each person is a unique expression of the energy. When I accept a Master Candidate, my job is to walk along side and support that Candidate to find, and live, the Mastery within, through Reiki. We both get to practice the Principles - a lot. The effort? As much as it takes. The time factor? As long as it takes. The rewards? Beyond description.

All blessings on your path.

Namaste -

Penelope Jewell
November 1, 1995
Edited and updated 27 January 1998

An Open Letter to Reiki Practitioners and Sharing Groups:

Thank you for inviting me to share Reiki with you. I travel around quite a bit and I notice that Reiki practice and sharing groups can be very different. Thank you for taking a moment to verbalize the etiquette of your group so we can be sure we are all in agreement about Reiki practice within those bounds, whatever they may be. I feel quite vulnerable in a prone position. I like to know what is happening before I lie down and surrender myself to your caring hands.

Just Reiki Please -

Is it Reiki that we are doing? I'm a purist and I like my Reiki straight. Please don't drape me in crystals, drip coloured oils upon my head, or chant exotic phrases over my body. I'd love to sample your other modes of healing, but not with, or instead of Reiki, when Reiki is what I'm expecting.

My body is the one that draws Reiki to fill its own needs, so please don't try to manipulate or direct the energy. I used to do psychic healing myself, and I gave it up for Reiki because I like Reiki better. And please don't call in any entities or deities to assist in my healing. We may not be familiar or compatible with each other. Reiki is wiser than any of us. If you have been properly initiated into Reiki, you are sufficient to the task of giving this treatment, I assure you. And I am sufficient to receive it and use it for my highest good.

The Time Factor -

Are we doing full treatments, no matter how long each person takes, or are we dividing up available time among practitioners and tables? If we are dividing time, are we all here, or do some people arrive late? Are you serious about the beginning and ending times, or are we likely to start late or run over? I may have another appointment, or need to arrange a ride. Have we set aside our differences and agreed upon a form for treatment? Are we using uniform positions held for uniform amounts of time, or are we placing hands wherever we feel called and moving whenever we wish?

Choices -

Do I have a choice about who works with me, or what areas of my body I would like to have worked on? If I have a choice about body parts, I'd like group time Reiki on my back, I can reach everywhere else! Are we placing hands on the body, or are we working in the aura, or do we all do our own thing?

I prefer everyone's hands on my body, please, with a tissue over my eyes, a pillow under my knees, and a blanket if those things are available. Laughter is great, but it can feel more like a massage than a Reiki treatment if the giggles get the best of us. I promise not to escape if you promise not to exert undue pressure, a light hands-on is fine, with no poking, prodding, or sudden movements that surprise me after I'm relaxed.

Music or Not -

If you intend to play music, may we discuss it first? Magnificent and supportive to you may be distracting or discordant to me and vice versa, so let's just check, OK? Also, we may need to adjust the volume after everyone quiets down. Are the telephones unplugged, or is there one ready to go off under the table? How about dish/clothes washers, TV's radios, alarm clocks, electronic watches or equipment? In general I prefer machine things unplugged, disengaged, and peacefully silent.

Speaking of noise are we a chatty or a silent group? I may or may not know the people you are talking about, and I might not want Aunt Frieda's gall bladder attack replayed over my head treatment. I'd love to hear about your latest operation, but later, please. While we are at it, please don't diagnose any diseases for me, especially when I am lying down. I'd rather not have those seeds planted in my subconscious when I am in an altered state. At least wait until I am sitting up with my shoes on to discuss any concerns. I am better able to handle it then.

Smells of the Day -

Speaking of things that come across stronger when I am lying down, that cologne you got for Christmas is lovely, but thanks for wearing less rather than more. I love the smell of incense, but three sticks is too much for easy breathing. Thanks for "cleansing" the room earlier in the day. I love the smell of good tobacco, but not second hand. The same for foods like garlic, onions, and some cheeses. Thanks for washing up before we start.

A Few Other Concerns -

Speaking of washing hands, if you have an active cold or the flu, I'll be glad to come back another time, but if you are just blowing your nose or performing other body functions, I'll be gland to wait until you have finished and washed your hands again, thanks. By the way, where is the bathroom and the light within? Is there anything I need to know about operating the toilet, or not? Is there water available to drink, tap or bottle, and clean glasses?

I love cats and dogs and children, but not on me when I am giving or receiving Reiki, unless I've agreed to that at the start. Are the windows open or closed, the fan and lights off or on, the temperature up or down, and are these negotiable items? I appreciate your offer of lengthy philosophical conversation - another time, if you don't mind. And this really isn't the time to try to sell me your used car, stock options, or a partnership in your latest venture.

On My End Of It -

I'd like to promise you a few things. I promise not to wear, or to remove before I lie down, any clothing, jewelry, heavy make-up, oils or lotions that could damage your sheets or table. I promise to take my own advice about strong odors in close quarters, and to wash my socks every once in a while, so as not to offend. I can't promise not to snore, but you get a gold star if I do.

If you are at my home I promise to take my own advice about telephones and faxes, and assure you I won't interrupt our treatment to answer them. I do have dogs and cats and children, but unless there is an emergency, they are fairly well behaved and won't interrupt us either.

If I am paying for this treatment, I promise to do so before we start, and not to require you to chase after me to ask for payment as I am leaving. I promise not to linger an unreasonable amount of time after the sharing/treatment is over. I realize you are on a schedule, too.

Thank you for your time, and for offering me a cup of tea or a glass of water before I leave. I'll do the same for you.

Most of all, thanks for sharing Reiki with me!

Namaste -

Penelope Jewell

RECOMMENDED READING

Reiki:

Reiki, Universal Life Energy, Bodo J. Baginski and Shalila Sharamon

Reiki Energy Medicine, Libby Barnett and Maggie Chambers

Living Reiki, Takata's Teachings, as told by Fran Brown

Reiki and Medicine, Nancy Eos, M.D.

Reiki in Everyday Living: How Universal Energy is a Natural Part of Life, Medicine, and Personal Growth, Earlene F. Gleisner

Reiki, Hawayo Takata's Story, Helen J. Haberly

Empowerment Through Reiki, Paula Horan

Abundance Through Reiki, Paula Horan

Complete Book of Reiki Healing Brigitte Muller & Horst H. Gunther

Reiki Fire by Frank Petter

In the Light of a Distant Star, Wanja Twan

Notes on Reiki The Usui System of Natural Healing, Carol von Kaenel

Others:

Anything by:

Deepak Chopra
Brook Medicine Eagle
Louise L. Hay
Eagle Man Ed McGaa
Catherine Ponder
Florence Scoval Shinn
Bernie S. Siegel, MD

BIBLIOGRAPHY

Baginski, B. J.& Sharamon, S., *Reiki: Universal Life Energy.* (C. Baker & J. Harrison, translators) Mendocino, Ca: Life Rhythm, 1988. (Orig. published 1985.)

Brown, Fran, *Living Reiki, Takata's Teachings.* Mendocino, Ca: Life Rhythm 1992.

Carper, J., *Food - Your Miracle Medicine.* New York: Harper Collins 1993.

Cooley, D.G. (Ed.). *Better Homes and Gardens Family Medical Guide* (Rev. ed.). New York: Better Homes and Gardens Books, 1976.

Hay, L.L., *Heal Your Body*, (Exp. and rev. ed.). Carson, CA: Hay House Inc., 1992.

Horan, P., *Empowerment Through Reiki.* Wilmot, WI: Lotus Light, 1992.

Jackson, S., *Anatomy and Physiology for Nurses.* London: Balliere Tindall, 1979. (Originally published 1939.)

Jewell, P., *Reiki Teaching Notes.* Unpublished. 1989.

Kapit, W., & Elson, L. M., *The Anatomy Coloring Book*, New York: HarperCollins Publishers, 1977.

Kapit, W., Macey, R. I., & Meisami, E., *The Physiology Coloring Book.* New York: HarperCollins Publishers, 1987.

Mackean, D. G., *Human Life.* London: John Murray (Publishers) Ltd., 1993. (Originally published, 1988.)

Minett, P., Wayne, D., Rubenstein, D., *Human Form and Function* London: Collins Educational, HarperCollins Publishers, 1994. (Orig. publ. 1989 Unwin Hyman Ltd.)

Parker, S., *The Body Atlas.* London: Dorling Kindersley, Inc., 1993

Ponder, Catherine, *The Dynamic Laws of Prosperity*, Marina del Rey, California: DeVorss & Company, 1990

Rick, S., *The Reflexology Workout.* New York: Harmony Books, Crown Publishers, 1986.

vonKaenel, C., *Notes on Reiki The Usui System of Natural Healing and Other Interesting Subjects.* New York: vonKaenel Productions, 1994

Namaste-

I honor the place within you in which the entire Universe dwells.

I honor the place within you which is of love, of truth, of light and of peace.

When you are in that place in you, and I am in that place in me,

We are One

Order Form

Reiki: A Guide to Your Practice of Reiki Energy Healing

All books are also available on-line at http://www.adirondackpress.com.

A Teaching version is also available in an unbound 3-hole punched printing. Quantity purchases for both versions are discounted, for pricing:

Contact the publisher at:

Email:	publisher@adirondackpress.com
Web:	www.adirondackpress.com
Phone:	(518) 330-3060
Mail:	Adirondack Press, Inc.
	678 Troy Schenectady Rd., Suite 104
	Latham, NY 12110

- -

Name:		**Date:**	
Address:			
City:	**State:**	**Zip:**	
**Telephone: ( ) - **		**Email:**	

Qty:	Description:	Price:	Total:
	Reiki: A Guide to Your Practice of Reiki Energy Healing	$18.50	
	Unbound 3-whole punched teaching version	$15.50	
	Subtotal		
	Sales Tax for NYS residents only – add 8%		
	Shipping and Handling $3.00 plus $1.50 per each additional book. $6.00 for International orders plus $2.00 for each additional book.		
	Total		

Mail this form with a check or money order to:
(Credit Card orders are taken over the website: http://www.adirondackpress.com)

Adirondack Press, Inc.
678 Troy Schenectady Road, Suite 104
Latham, New York 12110